Marketing essentials for StartUps

Marketing essentials for StartUps

How to build your brand
and drive business growth

Pablo Conrad

Pablo Conrad
June 2024

ISBN 979-8-3274-0849-4

Independently published,
The Woodlands, Texas, USA

Chapters content breakdown:

This book is dedicated with love to :

my wife, Luz María

my son, Santiago

my daughter, Belén

Who constantly inspire me to do my best

Preface:

I have been a marketer for almost three decades now. Over the years, I have learned the importance of understanding markets, segments, and customer needs before making any recommendations to address them. I have applied fundamental marketing principles such as Segmentation, Targeting and Positioning, The Marketing Funnel, The 4 P's (Product, Price, Place, and Promotion), and the role of Brands.

Throughout my career, I have designed and implemented Brand Strategies, Channel Strategies, and Pricing Strategies across various categories, sectors, and markets worldwide. After leaving the corporate world, I have dedicated my time to supporting startups in their ambitions to grow their businesses in diverse industries and markets.

During this period, I have realized two critical insights:

1. Many of the concepts I had fully embraced and assumed were common knowledge were not so obvious to many intelligent entrepreneurs.
2. Many entrepreneurs do not have the time (or patience) to focus on the fundamentals of Marketing, which can lead to painful and costly mistakes down the road for the success of their companies.

This realization led me to create this simple book as a guide for smart people with limited time. It aims to provide clarity on what to do first, what to focus on when thinking about marketing, and how to grow your brand and business effectively.

I hope you find this book useful, enjoyable, and that you will share your feedback with me to improve it for other entrepreneurs like you.

Enjoy the reading!

Chapter 1: Introduction to Startup Marketing

In the dynamic world of startups, marketing serves as the lifeblood that propels an idea from obscurity to prominence. The essence of startup marketing lies in its ability to create value for customers, build brand awareness, and foster sustainable growth. Unlike established enterprises, startups often operate with limited resources and face unique challenges that require innovative and cost-effective marketing strategies. This chapter will delve into the fundamentals of startup marketing, emphasizing the critical role it plays in the success of new ventures.

Marketing for startups is not just about promoting products or services; it's about understanding the market landscape, identifying customer needs, and delivering solutions that resonate. At its core, marketing is about creating connections and building relationships. For startups, this means crafting a compelling narrative that captures the essence of their mission and vision. It's about telling a story that resonates with early adopters, investors, and potential partners.

One of the primary distinctions between startup marketing and traditional marketing is the emphasis on agility and adaptability. Startups operate in an environment characterized by rapid change and uncertainty. Therefore, marketing strategies must be flexible and responsive to evolving market conditions. This requires a deep understanding of the target audience and a willingness to pivot when necessary. Startups must embrace a test-and-learn approach, continuously experimenting with different tactics to discover what works best.

The Unique Challenges of Startup Marketing

Startups face several unique challenges that require a tailored marketing approach. These include limited budgets, lack of brand recognition, and the need for rapid growth. Understanding these challenges is the first step in developing effective marketing strategies.

1. Limited Budgets: Unlike established companies, startups often have limited marketing budgets. This constraint necessitates a focus on cost-effective strategies that deliver a high return on investment (ROI). Digital marketing, with its ability to target specific audiences and measure results, is often the preferred choice for startups.

2. Lack of Brand Recognition: Startups usually start from scratch with little or no brand recognition. Building a strong brand identity from the ground up is crucial for gaining customer trust and standing out in a crowded

market. This involves creating a compelling brand story and consistently communicating it across all channels.

3. Need for Rapid Growth: Startups typically operate under tight timelines, driven by investor expectations and competitive pressures. Rapid growth is essential for survival and success. This often involves a mix of aggressive customer acquisition strategies and scalable marketing practices.

Building a Strong Foundation

The foundation of effective startup marketing lies in a clear understanding of the market and the target audience. This involves conducting thorough market research, defining buyer personas, and developing a strong value proposition.

1. Market Research: Comprehensive market research helps startups understand the competitive landscape, identify market gaps, and uncover customer needs. This involves analyzing industry trends, studying competitors, and gathering customer insights through surveys, interviews, and focus groups.

2. Defining Buyer Personas: Creating detailed buyer personas helps startups understand their target audience's demographics, behaviors, and pain points. Personas guide marketing strategies and ensure that messages resonate with the intended audience.

3. Value Proposition: A compelling value proposition clearly articulates the unique benefits that a startup offers. It differentiates the startup from competitors and provides a persuasive reason for customers to choose its products or services.

Crafting a Compelling Brand Story

A strong brand story is essential for building emotional connections with customers. It humanizes the startup, conveys its mission and values, and creates a memorable impression. Crafting a compelling brand story involves several key elements:

1. Authenticity: Authenticity is crucial for building trust. Customers are more likely to connect with a brand that is genuine and transparent about its mission, values, and challenges.

2. Emotion: Emotion is a powerful driver of customer behavior. A compelling brand story evokes emotions, whether it's inspiration, empathy, or excitement. Emotional connections can turn customers into loyal advocates.

3. Narrative Structure: A good brand story follows a clear narrative structure, with a beginning, middle, and end. It starts with the startup's origin, highlights the challenges faced, and concludes with the impact made and the vision for the future.

Leveraging Digital Marketing Channels

Digital marketing offers cost-effective ways for startups to reach and engage with a broad audience. Key digital marketing channels include social media, search engine marketing, content marketing, and email marketing.

1. Social Media: Social media platforms like Facebook, Instagram, Twitter, and LinkedIn provide opportunities for startups to connect with their audience, share their brand story, and promote their products or services. Engaging content, regular interactions, and targeted ads can drive significant traffic and engagement.

2. Search Engine Marketing (SEM): SEM, including both search engine optimization (SEO) and pay-per-click

(PPC) advertising, helps startups increase their visibility on search engines like Google. SEO involves optimizing the website and content for relevant keywords, while PPC involves paying for ads that appear in search results.

3. Content Marketing: Creating valuable content that addresses the needs and interests of the target audience can attract and engage customers. This includes blog posts, videos, infographics, and white-papers. Content marketing establishes the startup as a thought leader and builds trust with the audience.

4. Email Marketing: Email marketing is a powerful tool for nurturing leads and maintaining relationships with customers. Personalized and targeted email campaigns can drive conversions and foster loyalty.

Measuring and Optimizing Marketing Efforts

Measuring the effectiveness of marketing efforts is crucial for continuous improvement. Startups should track key performance indicators (KPIs) such as website traffic, conversion rates, customer acquisition cost (CAC), and customer lifetime value (CLV). Analytics tools like Google Analytics and CRM systems can provide valuable insights.

1. Website Traffic: Analyzing website traffic helps startups understand how visitors find and interact with their website. This includes tracking sources of traffic (e.g., organic, paid, social), user behavior on the site, and conversion rates.

2. Conversion Rates: Tracking conversion rates helps startups measure the effectiveness of their marketing campaigns. This involves analyzing the percentage of visitors who take desired actions, such as making a purchase or signing up for a newsletter.

3. Customer Acquisition Cost (CAC): CAC measures the cost of acquiring a new customer. Reducing CAC while maintaining or increasing the quality of customers is essential for sustainable growth.

4. Customer Lifetime Value (CLV): CLV represents the total revenue a startup can expect from a customer over the course of their relationship. Increasing CLV through retention and upselling strategies is crucial for long-term success.

The Role of Innovation in Startup Marketing

Innovation is at the heart of successful startup marketing. Startups must constantly explore new ideas, experiment with different tactics, and adapt to changing market conditions. This involves a culture of continuous learning and improvement.

1. Experimentation: Startups should embrace a test-and-learn approach, where they continuously experiment with new marketing tactics. This could involve A/B testing different messages, trying new marketing channels, or launching pilot campaigns.

2. Adaptability: The ability to pivot and adapt to market feedback is crucial for startups. This involves being open to change and making data-driven decisions to refine marketing strategies.

3. Customer Feedback: Actively seeking and incorporating customer feedback helps startups improve their products and marketing efforts. This involves listening to customers through surveys, social media interactions, and direct communication.

In Conclusion

Startup marketing is a multifaceted discipline that requires creativity, strategic thinking, and a deep understanding of the target audience. By embracing a customer-centric approach, leveraging digital channels, and building a strong brand identity, startups can navigate the challenges of the market and achieve sustainable growth. As we delve deeper into the subsequent chapters, we will explore specific strategies and tactics that startups can use to build a successful marketing foundation and drive their business forward.

Chapter 1 Summary

In this chapter, we explored the fundamental principles of startup marketing, emphasizing the importance of creating value, building relationships, and adopting agile strategies. Understanding the unique challenges faced by startups, we delved into the critical role of branding, customer-centricity, and digital channels in driving growth.

Key Takeaways

- Agility and Adaptability: Startups must be flexible and responsive to changing market conditions, continuously experimenting with different marketing tactics.
- Customer-Centric Approach: Focus on understanding and meeting the needs of your target audience to build lasting relationships.
- Digital Channels: Leverage cost-effective digital marketing tools to reach a broad audience and amplify your message.

Chapter 2: Defining Your Brand

In the crowded and competitive startup ecosystem, a well-defined brand is a powerful asset that can differentiate a company and build a loyal customer base. Branding is more than just a logo or a catchy tagline; it encompasses the entire perception of a company and its products or services. This chapter will explore the essential elements of defining a brand, the importance of brand consistency, and the steps startups can take to establish a strong and memorable brand identity.

The Essence of Branding

At its core, a brand is a promise to customers. It conveys what they can expect from a company's products or services and how it differentiates from competitors. This promise is built on the startup's mission, vision, and values. Defining these foundational elements is the first step in creating a brand. The mission statement articulates the startup's purpose and the impact it aims to make. The vision statement provides a long-term perspective on what the startup aspires to achieve. Values represent the principles and beliefs that guide the startup's behavior and decision-making processes.

Mission and Vision

A strong brand begins with a clear mission and vision. The mission statement should succinctly explain why the startup exists, what it aims to achieve, and how it serves its customers. It should be specific, inspiring, and aligned with the startup's core values.

> Mission Statement Example:
>
> "To empower individuals with innovative fitness solutions that enhance their well-being and quality of life."
>
> The vision statement outlines the startup's long-term aspirations and what it hopes to become in the future. It should be forward-thinking, ambitious, and motivating for both employees and customers.
>
> Vision Statement Example:
>
> "To be the global leader in fitness technology, transforming lives through cutting-edge innovation and exceptional customer experiences."

Values

Values are the guiding principles that shape the startup's culture and decision-making. They define what the startup stands for and influence how it interacts with customers, employees, and stakeholders. Values should be authentic, actionable, and reflective of the startup's mission and vision.

Values Example:

1. Innovation: Continuously pushing the boundaries to develop groundbreaking solutions.
2. Integrity: Conducting business with honesty and transparency.
3. Customer-Centricity: Prioritizing the needs and satisfaction of our customers.
4. Excellence: Striving for the highest standards in everything we do.
5. Community: Building a supportive and inclusive environment.

Unique Selling Proposition (USP)

Once the foundational elements are in place, the next step is to identify the startup's unique selling proposition (USP). The USP is what sets the startup apart from its competitors and makes it appealing to its target audience. It could be an innovative product feature, exceptional customer service, or a compelling story. Understanding the USP helps in crafting a brand message that resonates with customers and communicates the startup's value proposition clearly and effectively.

USP Example:

"Our fitness app offers personalized workout plans and real-time feedback from certified trainers, providing users with a unique and interactive fitness experience."

Visual Identity

The visual identity of a brand, including the logo, color palette, typography, and imagery, plays a crucial role in how the brand is perceived. A well-designed logo should be simple, memorable, and reflective of the brand's personality. The color palette and typography should be consistent across all marketing materials to create a cohesive and recognizable look. Imagery, whether it's photography, illustrations, or graphics, should align with the brand's tone and style. Consistency in visual elements helps build brand recognition and reinforces the brand's identity in the minds of consumers.

1. Logo: The logo is the most recognizable element of a brand's visual identity. It should be distinctive and convey the essence of the brand. A well-designed logo can evoke emotions and create a lasting impression.

2. Color Palette: Colors have psychological effects and can influence how a brand is perceived. Choosing the right color palette is essential for conveying the brand's personality and values. For example, blue often represents trust and professionalism, while green symbolizes growth and health.

3. Typography: The choice of fonts should reflect the brand's character and be legible across various platforms. Consistent typography helps create a unified look and feel.

4. Imagery: Visual elements such as photos, illustrations, and graphics should be high-quality and consistent with the brand's style. Imagery can tell a story, evoke emotions, and enhance the overall brand experience.

Brand Voice and Tone

In addition to visual elements, the brand's voice and tone are critical components of its identity. The brand voice is the consistent expression of the brand through words and prose, while the tone can vary depending on the context and audience.

For example, a tech startup might use a friendly and approachable voice to make complex topics more accessible. The tone might be more formal in a whitepaper but more casual in social media posts. Developing a brand voice guide can help ensure that all communications reflect the brand's personality and values.

Voice and Tone Examples:

1. Voice: Friendly, knowledgeable, and empowering.
2. Tone:
    - Website Copy: Informative and professional.
    - Social Media Posts: Casual and engaging.
    - Customer Support: Supportive and empathetic.

Crafting a Compelling Brand Story

Building a strong brand also involves creating a compelling brand story. Storytelling is a powerful tool that can humanize a brand and create an emotional connection with the audience. The brand story should highlight the startup's journey, the challenges it has overcome, and the passion and dedication behind its products or services. Authenticity is key; the story should be genuine and resonate with the target audience's values and aspirations. By sharing its story, a startup can build trust and loyalty among customers.

1. Origin Story: Share the inspiration behind the startup's founding. What problem were the founders trying to solve? What motivated them to start the business?

2. Challenges and Triumphs: Discuss the obstacles the startup faced and how they were overcome. Highlighting challenges adds authenticity and relatability to the story.

3. Mission and Vision: Reinforce the startup's mission and vision within the narrative. Show how these guiding principles have shaped the startup's journey.

4. Customer Impact: Include testimonials or case studies that illustrate the positive impact the startup has had on its customers. Real-life examples add credibility and emotional resonance.

Ensuring Brand Consistency

Consistency is a hallmark of successful branding. It's important for startups to ensure that their brand is consistently represented across all touchpoints, from the website and social media channels to packaging and customer service interactions. Inconsistent branding can confuse customers and dilute the brand's impact. Startups should develop brand guidelines that outline the proper use of visual and verbal elements, ensuring that everyone in the organization, as well as external partners, adhere to the same standards.

1. Brand Guidelines: Create a comprehensive brand guide that includes rules for logo usage, color palette, typography, imagery, and voice. This document serves as a reference for maintaining brand consistency.

2. Training: Educate employees and partners on the importance of brand consistency and how to apply the brand guidelines in their work. Regular training sessions can reinforce these principles.

3. Quality Control: Implement processes to review and approve marketing materials and communications

before they are published. This helps ensure that all content aligns with the brand's standards.

Engaging with the Target Audience

Understanding and engaging with the target audience is crucial for building a strong brand. Startups need to conduct thorough market research to identify their ideal customers and understand their needs, preferences, and behaviors. This knowledge enables the startup to tailor its brand messaging and marketing efforts to resonate with the audience effectively. Engaging with customers through social media, surveys, and direct interactions can provide valuable insights and help build a community around the brand.

1. Market Research: Use surveys, interviews, and focus groups to gather insights into customer preferences and behaviors. Analyze data to identify trends and patterns.

2. Customer Segmentation: Divide the target audience into segments based on demographics, psychographics, and behaviors. This allows for more personalized and effective marketing.

3. Social Media Engagement: Actively engage with customers on social media platforms. Respond to comments, share user-generated content, and participate in conversations to build a community.

Adapting and Evolving the Brand

Brand evolution is a natural part of a startup's growth. As the startup matures and the market landscape changes, the brand may need to evolve to stay relevant and competitive. This could involve refreshing the visual identity, updating the brand messaging, or expanding the product line. However, any changes should be carefully considered and aligned with the brand's core values and mission to maintain authenticity and trust.

1. Rebranding: Consider rebranding if the current brand no longer aligns with the startup's vision or market position. This could involve a new logo, color palette, or messaging.

2. Brand Refresh: A brand refresh can involve subtle changes to update and modernize the brand without a complete overhaul. This could include new imagery, updated typography, or refined messaging.

3. Product Line Expansion: Expanding the product line can necessitate updates to the brand. Ensure that new products align with the brand's values and mission.

In Conclusion

Defining a brand is a strategic process that involves articulating the startup's mission, vision, and values, identifying its unique selling proposition, and creating a cohesive visual and verbal identity. Consistency, authenticity, and customer engagement are key to building a strong and memorable brand. As we move forward in this book, we will explore the practical aspects of market research, strategic planning, and other essential components of a successful marketing strategy for startups.

Chapter 2 Summary

This chapter covered the essential elements of defining a brand, including the mission, vision, values, and unique selling proposition (USP). We discussed the importance of a cohesive visual identity, brand voice, and compelling storytelling to create a strong brand presence.

Key Takeaways

- Foundational Elements: Clearly define your mission, vision, values, and USP to guide your branding efforts.
- Consistency: Ensure consistency in visual and verbal elements to build brand recognition and trust.
- Authentic Storytelling: Craft genuine stories that resonate with your audience and humanize your brand.

Chapter 3: Market Research and Analysis

Market research and analysis are critical components of a successful marketing strategy, especially for startups. Understanding the market landscape, customer needs, and competitive dynamics enables startups to make informed decisions and identify opportunities for growth. This chapter will explore the importance of market research, the different types of research methods, and the steps involved in conducting thorough market analysis.

The Importance of Market Research

Market research is the process of gathering, analyzing, and interpreting information about a market, including data on target customers, competitors, and industry trends. For startups, market research provides valuable insights that can guide product development, marketing strategies, and business planning. It helps startups understand the demand for their products or services, identify potential challenges, and uncover new opportunities.

1. Informed Decision-Making: Market research provides the data needed to make informed decisions. Whether it's launching a new product, entering a new market, or adjusting a marketing strategy, having reliable data ensures that decisions are based on evidence rather than intuition.

2. Identifying Opportunities: By understanding market trends and customer needs, startups can identify new opportunities for growth. This could involve targeting an underserved market segment, addressing unmet needs, or capitalizing on emerging trends.

3. Reducing Risks: Market research helps mitigate risks by providing insights into potential challenges and barriers to entry. Understanding the competitive landscape and customer preferences allows startups to anticipate and address potential issues.

Types of Market Research

There are two main types of market research: primary and secondary research. Each type has its own methods and applications, and they can be used in combination to gather comprehensive insights.

1. Primary Research: Primary research involves collecting original data directly from sources such as customers, prospects, and industry experts. This can be done through surveys, interviews, focus groups, and

observations. Primary research provides firsthand insights that are specific to the startup's needs and objectives.

- Surveys: Surveys are a common tool for collecting quantitative data from a large audience. They can be conducted online, via email, or in person, and can cover a wide range of topics, from customer satisfaction to purchasing habits.
- Interviews: Interviews provide qualitative insights through in-depth conversations with a smaller group of participants. These methods are useful for exploring attitudes, motivations, and perceptions in greater detail.
- Focus Groups: Focus groups involve guided discussions with a group of individuals from the target audience. They provide insights into group dynamics, opinions, and reactions to new ideas or products.
- Observations: Observational research involves watching how customers interact with products or services in real-life settings. This can provide valuable insights into user behavior and preferences.

2. Secondary Research: Secondary research involves analyzing existing data from sources such as industry reports, market studies, academic journals, and online databases. Secondary research is useful for gaining a broader understanding of the market and identifying trends and benchmarks.

    - Industry Reports: Reports published by market research firms and industry associations provide valuable data on market size, growth rates, and trends. They offer a macro-level view of the market landscape.

- Academic Journals: Academic studies and research papers provide insights into specific topics, theories, and methodologies. They can offer a deeper understanding of consumer behavior and market dynamics.
- Online Databases: Databases like Statista, IBISWorld, and Nielsen offer a wealth of data on various industries and markets. These resources provide access to statistical data, market forecasts, and consumer insights.
- Competitor Analysis: Analyzing competitors' websites, marketing materials, and financial reports can provide insights into their strategies, strengths, and weaknesses.

Steps in Conducting Market Research

The market research process involves several steps, from defining objectives to analyzing data. Each step is crucial for gathering accurate and actionable insights.

1. Define Research Objectives: Startups need to be clear about what they want to achieve with their research. This could include understanding customer preferences, evaluating market potential, assessing competitive strengths and weaknesses, or identifying new market segments. Clear objectives help in designing the research process and ensuring that the collected data is relevant and actionable.

2. Identify the Target Audience: Identifying the target audience involves segmenting the market based on demographic, psychographic, geographic, and behavioral factors. Understanding the characteristics and behaviors of different customer segments enables startups to tailor their marketing efforts and develop products or services that meet specific needs. For example, a tech startup might segment its market into tech-savvy millennials, small business owners, and

corporate clients, each with distinct preferences and pain points.

3. Choose Research Methods: With the target audience identified, startups can choose the appropriate research methods. Surveys are a common tool for collecting quantitative data from a large audience. Interviews and focus groups provide qualitative insights through in-depth conversations with a smaller group of participants. Observational research offers insights into actual user behavior. Secondary research can complement primary research by providing broader market context.

4. Data Collection: Data collection is a crucial phase of market research. Startups need to ensure that their data collection methods are reliable and unbiased. This involves designing clear and concise questions, using appropriate sampling techniques, and maintaining ethical standards. It's also important to gather data from a representative sample to ensure that the findings are generalizable to the larger population.

    - Sampling Techniques: Use random sampling to ensure that every member of the target population has an equal chance of being included. Stratified sampling can be used to ensure that specific subgroups are adequately represented.
    - Question Design: Ensure that survey questions are clear, unbiased, and relevant to the research objectives. Avoid leading questions and double-barreled questions that can confuse respondents.
    - Ethical Standards: Maintain confidentiality and obtain informed consent from participants. Ensure that data collection methods comply with legal and ethical guidelines.

5. Data Analysis: After collecting the data, the next step is data analysis. This involves organizing, processing, and interpreting the data to uncover patterns and insights. Quantitative data can be analyzed using statistical tools to identify trends, correlations, and differences between groups. Qualitative data, on the other hand, requires thematic analysis to identify common themes and insights. The goal of data analysis is to transform raw data into actionable insights that can inform decision-making.

   - Quantitative Analysis: Use statistical software like SPSS, SAS, or R to analyze survey data. Techniques such as regression analysis, factor analysis, and cluster analysis can provide deeper insights into relationships and patterns.
   - Qualitative Analysis: Use coding techniques to identify themes and patterns in interview transcripts and focus group discussions. Software like NVivo or Atlas.ti can assist in managing and analyzing qualitative data.

Key Outcomes of Market Research

One of the key outcomes of market research is the identification of customer needs and preferences. By understanding what customers value, startups can develop products and services that address those needs effectively. This customer-centric approach not only improves the chances of market acceptance but also builds loyalty and satisfaction.

1. Customer Needs and Preferences: Identify the core needs and preferences of the target audience. This can involve understanding pain points, desired features, and decision-making criteria. Insights into customer behavior and preferences can guide product development and marketing strategies.

2. Market Potential: Assess the overall market potential for the startup's products or services. This involves

estimating the size of the target market, identifying growth opportunities, and evaluating market saturation. Market potential analysis helps in setting realistic goals and expectations.

3. Competitive Analysis: Competitive analysis is another critical aspect of market research. Startups need to understand who their competitors are, what they offer, and how they position themselves in the market. This involves analyzing competitors' strengths and weaknesses, pricing strategies, marketing tactics, and customer reviews. Competitive analysis helps startups identify gaps in the market, differentiate their offerings, and develop strategies to gain a competitive edge.

4. Industry Trends: In addition to understanding customers and competitors, market research also involves analyzing industry trends and market dynamics. This includes tracking technological advancements, regulatory changes, economic conditions, and social trends that could impact the startup's business. Staying informed about industry developments enables startups to anticipate changes and adapt their strategies accordingly.

Using Market Research to Inform Strategy

Market research and analysis are indispensable tools for startups aiming to succeed in a competitive market. By gathering and analyzing data on customers, competitors, and industry trends, startups can make informed decisions, identify opportunities, and develop strategies that align with market needs.

1. Product Development: Use market research insights to guide product development. This involves designing products that meet customer needs, testing prototypes with target users, and iterating based on feedback. Market research can help identify features that are most

valued by customers and prioritize them in the development process.

2. Marketing Strategy: Inform marketing strategies with data-driven insights. This includes identifying the most effective channels to reach the target audience, crafting compelling messages that resonate with customers, and optimizing marketing campaigns based on performance data.

3. Sales Strategy: Tailor sales strategies based on customer insights and competitive analysis. This involves identifying key selling points, addressing common objections, and targeting high-potential customer segments. Market research can help sales teams understand customer needs and position the startup's offerings effectively.

4. Business Planning: Incorporate market research findings into business planning and strategy development. This involves setting realistic goals, identifying growth opportunities, and mitigating risks. Market research provides a solid foundation for making strategic decisions and achieving business objectives.

In Conclusion

In conclusion, market research and analysis are critical components of a successful marketing strategy for startups. By conducting thorough market research, startups can gain valuable insights into customer needs, market potential, and competitive dynamics. These insights inform decision-making, guide product development, and shape marketing strategies. As we move forward, we will explore how to translate these insights into strategic marketing plans that drive growth and success.

Chapter 3 Summary

We delved into the process of market research and analysis, highlighting the importance of understanding the market landscape, customer needs, and competitive dynamics. The chapter outlined primary and secondary research methods and the steps to conduct thorough market analysis.

Key Takeaways

- Define Objectives: Set clear research objectives to guide your market research efforts.
- Understand Your Audience: Create detailed buyer personas to tailor your marketing strategies effectively.
- Competitive Analysis: Continuously analyze competitors to identify market gaps and opportunities.

Chapter 4: Strategic Marketing Planning

Strategic marketing planning is the process of developing a comprehensive roadmap that outlines how a startup will achieve its marketing objectives and drive business growth. This chapter will guide you through the essential steps of creating a strategic marketing plan, including setting goals, analyzing the market, defining target audiences, developing marketing strategies, and measuring success.

Setting Clear, Measurable Goals

The first step in strategic marketing planning is to set clear, measurable, and achievable goals. These goals should align with the overall business objectives and provide a clear direction for the marketing efforts. Goals can be categorized into short-term and long-term objectives. Short-term goals might include increasing website traffic, generating leads, or boosting social media engagement, while long-term goals could focus on brand awareness, market penetration, or revenue growth. The SMART criteria—Specific, Measurable, Achievable, Relevant, and Time-bound—can be used to ensure that the goals are well-defined and attainable.

Examples of SMART Goals:

Increase Website Traffic: Increase website traffic by 30% within six months through a combination of SEO, content marketing, and social media strategies.

Generate Leads: Generate 500 new leads per month over the next year by optimizing lead capture forms and running targeted ad campaigns.

Boost Social Media Engagement: Achieve a 20% increase in social media engagement (likes, shares, comments) within three months by creating more interactive and shareable content.

Conducting a Thorough Market Analysis

Once the goals are established, the next step is to conduct a thorough market analysis. This involves examining the market landscape to understand the external factors that could impact the startup's success. A commonly used framework for this analysis is the PESTEL analysis, which examines Political, Economic, Social, Technological, Environmental, and Legal factors. Additionally, a SWOT analysis can help identify the startup's internal Strengths and Weaknesses, as well as external Opportunities and Threats. This comprehensive analysis provides valuable insights into the market conditions and helps in making informed strategic decisions.

PESTEL Analysis:

Political: Assess the impact of government policies, regulations, and political stability on the startup's operations and market potential.

Economic: Analyze economic factors such as inflation rates, economic growth, and consumer spending patterns that could influence market demand and pricing strategies.

Social: Understand social trends, demographics, and cultural factors that affect consumer behavior and preferences.

Technological: Evaluate technological advancements and innovations that could present opportunities or threats to the startup.

Environmental: Consider environmental factors such as sustainability trends and environmental regulations that could impact the startup's operations and reputation.

Legal: Identify legal and regulatory requirements that the startup must comply with, including industry-specific regulations and intellectual property laws.

SWOT Analysis:

Strengths: Identify the startup's internal strengths, such as unique product features, strong brand reputation, or a skilled team.

Weaknesses: Recognize internal weaknesses, such as limited resources, lack of market presence, or operational inefficiencies.

Opportunities: Explore external opportunities, such as emerging market trends, technological advancements, or gaps in the market that the startup can capitalize on.

Threats: Assess external threats, such as competitive pressures, regulatory changes, or economic downturns that could pose risks to the startup.

Defining the Target Audience

Defining the target audience is a critical component of strategic marketing planning. Startups need to identify the specific groups of customers they want to reach and understand their needs, preferences, and behaviors. This involves segmenting the market based on demographic, psychographic, geographic, and behavioral criteria. Creating detailed buyer personas can help visualize the ideal customers and tailor marketing messages to resonate with them. Each persona should include information such as age, gender, occupation, interests, pain points, and buying behavior.

Example Buyer Persona:

Name: Tech-Savvy Tom

Age: 28

Occupation: Software Developer

Location: Urban area

Interests: Technology, gadgets, coding, fitness

Pain Points: Limited time for workouts, looking for efficient fitness solutions

Buying Behavior: Prefers online shopping, relies on product reviews and recommendations

Developing Effective Marketing Strategies

With a clear understanding of the target audience, startups can develop effective marketing strategies. These strategies should outline how the startup plans to achieve its marketing goals and connect with its audience. Key components of the marketing strategy include:

Value Proposition: Clearly articulate the unique value that the startup offers to its customers. This should highlight the benefits and differentiators that set the startup apart from competitors.

Example Value Proposition:

> "Our fitness app offers personalized workout plans and real-time feedback from certified trainers, providing users with a unique and interactive fitness experience."

> Positioning: Define how the startup wants to be perceived in the market. This involves crafting a positioning statement that communicates the startup's unique attributes and the value it delivers to customers.

Example Positioning Statement:

"We are the go-to fitness app for busy professionals who want efficient, personalized workouts that fit into their hectic schedules."

Marketing Mix (4Ps): Develop a comprehensive plan for the marketing mix, which includes Product, Price, Place, and Promotion. This involves decisions about product features, pricing strategies, distribution channels, and promotional tactics.

Product: Define the key features, benefits, and unique selling points of the product or service.

Price: Establish pricing strategies that reflect the product's value and competitive positioning.

Place: Determine the distribution channels that will be used to reach the target audience, whether it's online, through retail partners, or direct sales.

Promotion: Plan promotional activities that will raise awareness, generate interest, and drive sales. This could include advertising, public relations, social media campaigns, and content marketing.

Channels: Identify the most effective channels for reaching the target audience. This could include digital channels such as social media, email marketing, search engine optimization (SEO), and content marketing, as well as traditional channels like events, partnerships, and public relations.

Channel Strategy Example:

Social Media: Utilize platforms like Instagram and Facebook to engage with the target audience through regular posts, stories, and ads.

Email Marketing: Send personalized email campaigns to nurture leads and keep existing customers informed about new features and promotions.

SEO: Optimize the website and blog content to rank higher in search engine results for relevant keywords.

Content Marketing: Create valuable content such as blog posts, videos, and infographics that address the target audience's interests and pain points.

Content and Messaging: Develop a content strategy that aligns with the startup's brand and resonates with the target audience. This includes creating valuable and engaging content that addresses customer needs and reinforces the startup's value proposition.

Content Strategy Example:

> Blog Posts: Publish weekly blog posts on topics related to fitness, health, and wellness.

Videos: Create tutorial videos demonstrating workout routines and fitness tips.

Social Media Content: Share user-generated content, success stories, and behind-the-scenes looks at the startup's journey.

Budget and Resources: Allocate the necessary budget and resources to execute the marketing plan. This involves estimating costs for various marketing activities and ensuring that the startup has the tools and talent needed to implement the strategies effectively.

Budget Allocation Example:

Digital Advertising: $5,000 per month for social media ads and PPC campaigns.

Content Creation: $2,000 per month for blog posts, videos, and graphics.

Software Tools: $1,000 per month for marketing automation and analytics tools.

Measuring and Evaluating Success

Measurement and evaluation are essential to ensure that the marketing plan is delivering the desired results. Startups should establish key performance indicators (KPIs) to track progress towards their goals. KPIs could include metrics such as website traffic, conversion rates, customer acquisition cost (CAC), and return on investment (ROI). Regularly monitoring these metrics allows startups to assess the effectiveness of their marketing efforts and make data-driven adjustments as needed.

Website Traffic: Track the number of visitors to the startup's website and analyze their behavior. Use tools like Google Analytics to monitor page views, bounce rates, and time spent on the site.

Conversion Rates: Measure the percentage of website visitors who complete a desired action, such as signing up for a newsletter or making a purchase. Optimize landing pages and calls to action (CTAs) to improve conversion rates.

Customer Acquisition Cost (CAC): Calculate the total cost of acquiring a new customer, including marketing and sales expenses. Aim to reduce CAC over time by improving the efficiency of marketing campaigns.

Return on Investment (ROI): Assess the financial return generated from marketing efforts relative to the cost. Use ROI calculations to evaluate the profitability of different marketing activities and allocate budget accordingly.

Customer Lifetime Value (CLV): Estimate the total revenue a startup can expect from a customer over the course of their relationship. Focus on increasing CLV through retention strategies and upselling opportunities.

Flexibility and Adaptability

A crucial aspect of strategic marketing planning is flexibility and adaptability. The market environment is constantly changing, and startups need to be agile in responding to new opportunities and challenges. This involves continuously analyzing market trends, gathering feedback from customers, and testing different marketing tactics. Startups should be prepared to pivot their strategies when necessary to stay aligned with their goals and market conditions.

Continuous Monitoring: Regularly review marketing performance data and market trends to identify changes and emerging opportunities. Use this information to make timely adjustments to the marketing plan.

Customer Feedback: Actively seek feedback from customers through surveys, reviews, and direct interactions. Use this feedback to refine marketing messages, improve products, and enhance the customer experience.

A/B Testing: Conduct A/B tests on various elements of marketing campaigns, such as email subject lines, ad creatives, and landing page designs. Use the results to optimize campaigns for better performance.

Agile Marketing: Adopt an agile marketing approach that allows for rapid experimentation and iteration. Create short-term marketing plans that can be quickly adjusted based on results and feedback.

In Conclusion

Strategic marketing planning is a dynamic and ongoing process that requires a clear understanding of the market, a deep knowledge of the target audience, and a well-defined strategy to achieve marketing goals. By setting clear objectives, conducting thorough market analysis, defining target audiences, developing effective strategies, and measuring success, startups can build a strong foundation for sustainable growth. As we move to the next chapter, we will explore the basics of digital marketing and how startups can leverage digital channels to reach and engage with their audience.

Chapter 4 Summary

This chapter focused on developing a comprehensive strategic marketing plan, including setting goals, analyzing the market, defining target audiences, and developing marketing strategies. We also emphasized the importance of measurement and continuous optimization.

Key Takeaways

- Set Clear Goals: Define specific, measurable, and achievable marketing objectives.
- Data-Driven Strategies: Use market analysis to inform your strategic decisions.
- Continuous Optimization: Regularly monitor and adjust your marketing efforts based on performance metrics.

Chapter 5: Digital Marketing Basics

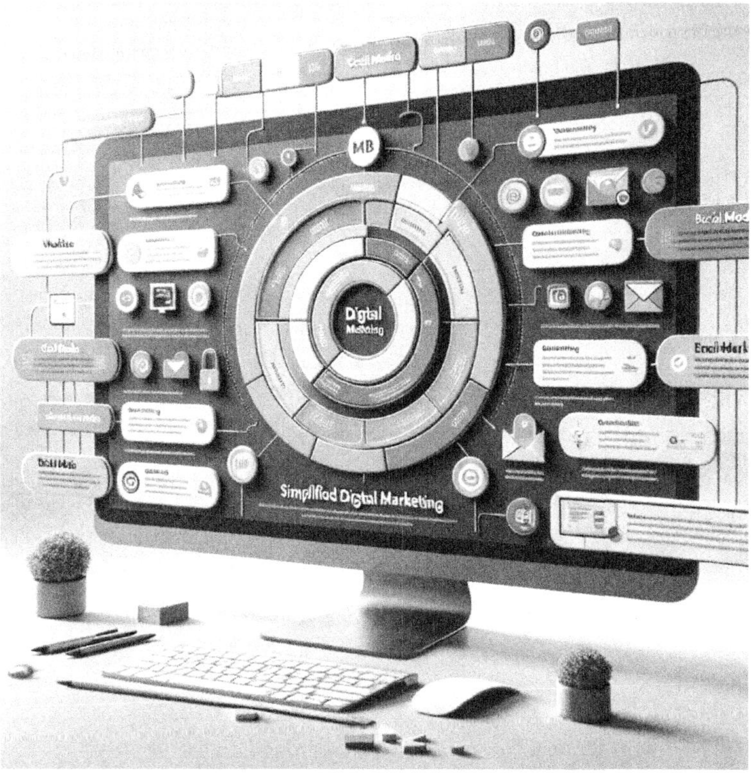

In the digital age, effective marketing is synonymous with digital marketing. For startups, mastering the basics of digital marketing is crucial for building an online presence, reaching a wider audience, and driving growth. This chapter will cover the fundamental concepts of digital marketing, including search engine optimization (SEO), content marketing, social media marketing, email marketing, and pay-per-click (PPC) advertising.

Overview of Digital Marketing

Digital marketing encompasses all marketing efforts that use the internet or electronic devices. It leverages various online channels such as search engines, social media, email, and websites to connect with current and prospective customers. Unlike traditional marketing, digital marketing offers unparalleled opportunities for targeting, personalization, and measuring results in real-time.

Targeting: Digital marketing allows startups to target specific audiences based on demographics, interests, and behaviors. This precision targeting ensures that marketing messages reach the right people at the right time.

Personalization: Personalization involves tailoring marketing messages and content to individual preferences. Digital marketing platforms enable startups to deliver personalized experiences that resonate with customers.

Measurement: Digital marketing provides access to detailed analytics and performance data. Startups can track metrics such as website traffic, conversion rates, and customer engagement to measure the effectiveness of their campaigns.

Search Engine Optimization (SEO)

Search engine optimization (SEO) is the process of optimizing a website to rank higher in search engine results pages (SERPs) for relevant keywords. Higher rankings lead to increased visibility and organic traffic. SEO involves several components:

Keyword Research: Identifying the keywords and phrases that potential customers use to search for products or services related to the startup. Tools like Google Keyword Planner, Ahrefs, and SEMrush can help in finding the right keywords.

Example Keywords for a Fitness App:

"personalized workout plans"

"fitness app for busy professionals"

"real-time fitness feedback"

On-Page SEO: Optimizing individual web pages to rank higher and earn more relevant traffic. This includes using targeted keywords in the title tags, meta descriptions, headers, and content, as well as optimizing images and improving site speed.

On-Page SEO Checklist:

Title Tags: Include primary keywords and keep titles under 60 characters.

Meta Descriptions: Write compelling descriptions that include keywords and are under 160 characters.

Headers (H1, H2, H3): Use headers to structure content and include relevant keywords.

Content: Ensure content is high-quality, relevant, and includes keywords naturally.

Images: Optimize images with descriptive file names and alt text.

Site Speed: Improve loading times by compressing images, using a content delivery network (CDN), and minimizing code.

Off-Page SEO: Building the website's authority and trustworthiness through activities outside the website. This primarily involves earning backlinks from reputable sites, which signal to search engines that the website is a credible source of information.

Off-Page SEO Strategies:

Link Building: Earn backlinks by creating valuable content that others want to link to, such as guest posts, infographics, and research reports.

Social Media: Promote content on social media platforms to increase visibility and attract links.

Influencer Outreach: Collaborate with influencers and industry experts to generate high-quality backlinks.

Technical SEO: Ensuring that the website is structured in a way that search engines can crawl and index it effectively. This includes optimizing the site's architecture, using schema markup, and ensuring a mobile-friendly design.

Technical SEO Best Practices:

Site Architecture: Use a logical structure with clear navigation and internal linking.

Schema Markup: Implement schema markup to help search engines understand the content.

Mobile Optimization: Ensure the website is responsive and provides a good user experience on mobile devices.

Content Marketing

Content marketing involves creating and distributing valuable, relevant, and consistent content to attract and engage a clearly defined audience. The goal is to drive profitable customer action by providing content that addresses the audience's needs and interests. Content marketing includes blog posts, articles, videos, infographics, podcasts, and more.

Key Aspects of Content Marketing:

Content Strategy: Developing a plan for creating and sharing content that aligns with the startup's goals and audience preferences. This involves setting objectives, identifying topics, and choosing the right formats and channels.

Content Strategy Examplé:

Objective: Increase brand awareness and drive website traffic.

Topics: Fitness tips, workout routines, nutrition advice, success stories.

Formats: Blog posts, videos, infographics, social media posts.

Channels: Website, YouTube, Instagram, email newsletters.

Content Creation: Producing high-quality content that provides value to the audience. This means focusing on informative, entertaining, or educational content that addresses the pain points and interests of the target audience.

Content Creation Tips:

Research: Conduct thorough research to ensure content is accurate and informative.

Storytelling: Use storytelling techniques to make content engaging and relatable.

Visuals: Incorporate images, videos, and graphics to enhance the content and improve readability.

Content Distribution: Sharing content through various channels to reach the target audience. This could include the startup's website, social media platforms, email newsletters, and guest posts on other websites.

Content Distribution Channels:

Website: Publish blog posts and articles on the company's website.

Social Media: Share content on platforms like Facebook, Twitter, Instagram, and LinkedIn.

Email Newsletters: Send content directly to subscribers through regular email campaigns.

Guest Posting: Contribute articles to industry blogs and websites to reach a wider audience.

Content Optimization: Ensuring that content is optimized for search engines and user engagement. This involves using relevant keywords, crafting compelling headlines, and incorporating multimedia elements.

Content Optimization Techniques:

Keyword Integration: Use primary and secondary keywords naturally within the content.

Headlines: Write attention-grabbing headlines that include keywords and spark interest.

Multimedia: Add images, videos, and infographics to make content more engaging and shareable.

Social Media Marketing

Social media marketing uses social media platforms to connect with the audience, build the brand, and drive traffic and sales. It involves creating and sharing content on social media networks like Facebook, Instagram, Twitter, LinkedIn, and others.

Key Components of Social Media Marketing:

Platform Selection: Choosing the right social media platforms based on where the target audience spends their time. Each platform has its unique demographics and content formats.

Platform Selection Guide:

Facebook: Wide demographic reach, suitable for a variety of content types.

Instagram: Visual platform, ideal for photos and short videos.

Twitter: Real-time updates, great for news and short-form content.

LinkedIn: Professional network, best for B2B marketing and thought leadership.

Content Planning: Developing a content calendar that outlines what content will be posted, when, and on which platforms. Consistency is crucial for building and maintaining engagement.

Content Calendar Example:

Monday: Motivational quote and fitness tip on Instagram.

Wednesday: Blog post link and discussion prompt on Facebook.

Friday: User-generated content and success story on Twitter.

Engagement: Actively interacting with followers by responding to comments, messages, and mentions. This helps build a community around the brand and fosters customer loyalty.

Engagement Best Practices:

Respond Promptly: Reply to comments and messages in a timely manner.

Encourage Interaction: Ask questions, run polls, and invite followers to share their experiences.

Show Appreciation: Acknowledge and thank followers for their support and contributions.

Analytics: Tracking social media metrics such as likes, shares, comments, and clicks to measure the effectiveness of social media efforts. Tools like Facebook Insights, Twitter Analytics, and Hootsuite can provide valuable data.

Social Media Metrics to Track:

Engagement Rate: The percentage of followers who interact with content.

Reach: The number of unique users who see the content.

Impressions: The total number of times content is displayed.

Click-Through Rate (CTR): The percentage of users who click on a link in the post.

Email Marketing

Email marketing involves sending targeted messages to a group of subscribers via email. It's a powerful way to nurture leads, build relationships, and drive conversions.

Key Elements of Email Marketing:

Email List Building: Growing a list of subscribers who have opted in to receive communications from the startup. This can be done through sign-up forms, landing pages, and lead magnets.

Email List Building Techniques:

Sign-Up Forms: Place sign-up forms on the website, blog, and social media profiles.

Lead Magnets: Offer valuable incentives such as eBooks, checklists, or discounts in exchange for email addresses.

Landing Pages: Create dedicated landing pages with compelling offers to capture email leads.

Email Campaigns: Creating and sending emails that provide value to subscribers. This could include newsletters, promotional offers, product updates, and personalized recommendations.

Types of Email Campaigns:

Newsletters: Regular updates on company news, blog posts, and industry insights.

Promotions: Special offers, discounts, and limited-time deals.

Product Updates: Announcements about new features, products, or services.

Personalized Recommendations: Tailored product suggestions based on user behavior and preferences.

Segmentation: Dividing the email list into smaller segments based on criteria such as demographics, behavior, and past interactions. This allows for more personalized and relevant email content.

Segmentation Strategies:

Demographics: Segment based on age, gender, location, or job title.

Behavior: Segment based on past purchase behavior, website activity, or email engagement.

Preferences: Segment based on user preferences and interests collected through surveys or sign-up forms.

Analytics: Measuring the performance of email campaigns using metrics like open rates, click-through rates, and conversion rates. This helps in optimizing future campaigns for better results.

Email Marketing Metrics to Track:

Open Rate: The percentage of recipients who open the email.

Click-Through Rate (CTR): The percentage of recipients who click on a link within the email.

Conversion Rate: The percentage of recipients who complete a desired action, such as making a purchase or filling out a form.

Unsubscribe Rate: The percentage of recipients who opt out of the email list.

Pay-Per-Click (PPC) Advertising

Pay-per-click (PPC) advertising is a model of internet marketing where advertisers pay a fee each time one of their ads is clicked. It's a way of buying visits to the website rather than earning them organically.

Key Aspects of PPC Advertising:

Keyword Research: Identifying the keywords for which the startup wants its ads to appear. These should be relevant to the products or services offered.

Keyword Research Tools:

Google Keyword Planner: Find relevant keywords and estimate search volumes.

SEMrush: Analyze competitor keywords and discover new keyword opportunities.

Ahrefs: Track keyword rankings and explore keyword ideas.

Ad Creation: Crafting compelling ads that attract clicks. This includes writing engaging ad copy, choosing the right visuals, and designing landing pages that convert.

Ad Creation Tips:

Ad Copy: Write clear and persuasive ad copy that highlights the unique selling points and includes a strong call to action (CTA).

Visuals: Use high-quality images or videos that capture attention and reinforce the message.

Landing Pages: Ensure landing pages are relevant to the ad, provide value, and have a clear CTA.

Bid Management: Setting and managing bids for ad placements to ensure the startup's ads appear in favorable positions without overspending.

Bid Management Strategies:

Manual Bidding: Manually set bids for keywords based on performance and budget.

Automated Bidding: Use automated bidding strategies provided by ad platforms to optimize bids for specific goals, such as maximizing clicks or conversions.

Analytics: Tracking and analyzing the performance of PPC campaigns using metrics like cost per click (CPC), click-through rate (CTR), and return on ad spend (ROAS).

PPC Metrics to Track:

Cost Per Click (CPC): The average cost of each click on the ad.

Click-Through Rate (CTR): The percentage of ad impressions that result in clicks.

Conversion Rate: The percentage of clicks that result in a desired action, such as a purchase or sign-up.

Return on Ad Spend (ROAS): The revenue generated for every dollar spent on PPC advertising.

Integrating Digital Marketing Channels

Integrating various digital marketing channels can amplify the effectiveness of marketing efforts and create a cohesive brand experience. A multi-channel approach ensures that the startup reaches its audience through different touchpoints and maximizes engagement.

Integration Strategies:

Unified Messaging: Ensure consistent messaging and branding across all digital channels.

Cross-Promotion: Promote content and campaigns across multiple channels to increase visibility and reach.

Customer Journey Mapping: Understand the customer journey and create integrated marketing strategies that guide customers from awareness to conversion.

In Conclusion

Digital marketing is a multifaceted discipline that requires a strategic approach and a deep understanding of various online channels. By mastering the basics of SEO, content marketing, social media marketing, email marketing, and PPC advertising, startups can build a strong online presence, engage with their audience, and drive growth. As we continue, we will delve into the art of content marketing and storytelling, exploring how startups can create compelling narratives that resonate with their audience.

Chapter 5 Summary

We explored the fundamental concepts of digital marketing, including SEO, content marketing, social media marketing, email marketing, and PPC advertising. The chapter emphasized the importance of leveraging digital channels to reach and engage a wider audience.

Key Takeaways

- SEO Fundamentals: Optimize your website to rank higher in search engine results and drive organic traffic.
- Content Marketing: Create valuable content that addresses the needs of your audience.
- Multi-Channel Approach: Utilize various digital channels to amplify your reach and impact

Chapter 6: Content Marketing and Storytelling

In the world of digital marketing, content is king. Content marketing is the strategic approach of creating and distributing valuable, relevant, and consistent content to attract and engage a clearly defined audience. For startups, content marketing is an essential tool for building brand awareness, establishing authority, and driving customer engagement. This chapter will explore the principles of content marketing and the power of storytelling, providing practical insights into how startups can craft compelling narratives that resonate with their audience.

The Essence of Content Marketing

Content marketing is about more than just producing content; it's about creating content that serves a purpose and provides value to the audience. The foundation of a successful content marketing strategy involves understanding the audience, setting clear objectives, and creating content that aligns with the brand's goals and values.

Understanding the Audience: The first step in content marketing is to deeply understand the target audience. This involves creating detailed buyer personas that outline the demographics, psychographics, needs, and pain points of the ideal customers. By knowing the audience, startups can create content that speaks directly to their interests and challenges.

Example Buyer Persona:

Name: Health-Conscious Hannah

Age: 32

Occupation: Marketing Manager

Location: Urban area

Interests: Healthy living, fitness, nutrition, mindfulness

Pain Points: Balancing work and wellness, finding reliable health information

Buying Behavior: Prefers organic products, follows health influencers, values expert advice

Setting Objectives: Content marketing objectives should align with the overall business and marketing goals. Common objectives include increasing brand awareness, generating leads, nurturing customer relationships, and driving sales. Clear objectives help guide the content creation process and ensure that each piece of content serves a strategic purpose.

Example Objectives:

Increase Brand Awareness: Publish blog posts and videos that showcase the startup's expertise in fitness and wellness.

Generate Leads: Create downloadable resources (e.g., eBooks, checklists) that require users to provide their email addresses.

Nurture Customer Relationships: Send regular newsletters with valuable content to keep subscribers engaged.

Drive Sales: Develop product-focused content that highlights features, benefits, and customer testimonials.

Content Creation: Creating high-quality content that provides value to the audience is at the heart of content marketing. This can take many forms, including blog posts, articles, videos, infographics, podcasts, webinars, and more. The key is to produce content that is informative, entertaining, or educational and that addresses the audience's needs and interests.

Content Types:

Blog Posts: Regularly updated articles that provide valuable information and insights on relevant topics.

Videos: Engaging visual content that can demonstrate product use, provide tutorials, or share customer stories.

Infographics: Visually appealing graphics that present data and information in an easily digestible format.

Podcasts: Audio content that can feature interviews, discussions, and expert advice on industry topics.

Webinars: Live or recorded online seminars that offer in-depth exploration of specific topics.

The Power of Storytelling

Storytelling is a powerful tool in content marketing. Stories have the ability to captivate audiences, evoke emotions, and create a memorable connection with the brand. For startups, storytelling can humanize the brand and differentiate it from competitors.

Elements of Effective Storytelling:

Authenticity: Authentic stories are genuine and resonate with the audience's values and experiences. Startups should share their journey, including the challenges they've faced, the passion behind their products or services, and the impact they aim to make. Authenticity builds trust and credibility.

Example Authentic Story:

"Our founder started this fitness app after struggling to find effective workout plans that fit into a busy schedule. She decided to create a solution that offers personalized plans and real-time feedback, helping people like her stay fit and healthy."

Emotional Connection: Stories that evoke emotions are more likely to be remembered and shared. Whether it's a story of overcoming adversity, a heartwarming customer success story, or an inspiring vision for the future, connecting with the audience on an emotional level helps build a loyal and engaged community.

Example Emotional Story:

"Meet John, a long-time user of our app. After a serious injury, John was unsure if he could ever get back to his fitness routine. With the help of our personalized plans and supportive community, John not only recovered but also achieved his fitness goals, inspiring others along the way."

Relatability: The best stories are those that the audience can relate to. By understanding the audience's needs and pain points, startups can craft stories that reflect their experiences and aspirations. This creates a sense of empathy and connection.

Example Relatable Story:

"Like many busy professionals, Sarah found it challenging to stick to a fitness routine. Our app provided Sarah with flexible workout plans that fit into her hectic schedule, helping her stay active and healthy without feeling overwhelmed."

Clarity and Simplicity: A compelling story is clear and easy to understand. It should have a beginning, middle, and end, with a clear message or takeaway. Avoid jargon and complexity; instead, focus on conveying the story in a straightforward and engaging manner.

Example Clear and Simple Story:

"Our mission is simple: to make fitness accessible and enjoyable for everyone. We started with a small idea and a big dream, and today, our app is helping thousands of people achieve their health goals, one step at a time."

Visual and Multimedia Elements: Incorporating visual and multimedia elements can enhance storytelling. Images, videos, infographics, and interactive content can bring the story to life and make it more engaging. Visual content is also more likely to be shared on social media, extending the reach of the story.

Example Multimedia Storytelling:

Video: Create a short documentary featuring real users sharing their fitness journeys and how the app has helped them.

Infographic: Design an infographic that illustrates the startup's growth and impact, using data and visuals to tell the story.

Interactive Content: Develop an interactive timeline on the website that showcases the startup's milestones and achievements.

Developing a Content and Storytelling Strategy

To effectively leverage content marketing and storytelling, startups need a strategic approach. Here are the key steps to developing a content and storytelling strategy:

Define the Brand Story: Start by defining the core story of the brand. This includes the mission, vision, and values, as well as the unique selling proposition (USP). The brand story should convey what the startup stands for and why it exists.

Example Brand Story:

"Our startup was born out of a passion for fitness and a desire to make healthy living accessible to everyone. Our mission is to empower individuals with personalized fitness solutions that fit into their busy lives. We believe in innovation, community, and excellence, and we are committed to helping our users achieve their health goals."

Create a Content Plan: Develop a content plan that outlines the types of content to be created, the topics to be covered, and the channels for distribution. The plan should align with the content marketing objectives and be tailored to the audience's preferences.

Example Content Plan:

Blog Posts: Weekly posts on fitness tips, nutrition advice, and workout routines.

Videos: Monthly video tutorials on different exercises and fitness techniques.

Social Media: Daily posts on Instagram and Facebook featuring user-generated content, motivational quotes, and success stories.

Email Newsletters: Bi-weekly newsletters with updates, special offers, and exclusive content.

Produce High-Quality Content: Focus on creating content that provides value and resonates with the audience. This involves conducting research, collaborating with experts, and investing in quality production. Consistency is key; regularly publishing high-quality content helps build credibility and authority.

Tips for High-Quality Content:

Research: Use credible sources and data to support the content.

Collaboration: Work with industry experts, influencers, and customers to create diverse and authoritative content.

Production: Invest in professional tools and resources to ensure high production quality.

Engage with the Audience: Engage with the audience by encouraging comments, feedback, and interactions. Responding to comments and messages, hosting Q&A sessions, and participating in online discussions helps build a community around the brand.

Engagement Strategies:

Interactive Posts: Create polls, quizzes, and Q&A sessions on social media.

User-Generated Content: Encourage users to share their experiences and feature them on the brand's platforms.

Community Building: Create online groups or forums where users can connect, share tips, and support each other.

Measure and Optimize: Track the performance of content using metrics such as website traffic, engagement rates, conversion rates, and social shares. Use these insights to optimize future content and storytelling efforts.

Content Performance Metrics:

Website Traffic: Monitor the number of visitors and page views on content pages.

Engagement Rates: Measure likes, shares, comments, and other interactions on social media.

Conversion Rates: Track the percentage of users who take desired actions, such as signing up for a newsletter or making a purchase.

Social Shares: Analyze how often content is shared on social media platforms.

In Conclusion

Content marketing and storytelling are essential components of a successful digital marketing strategy for startups. By understanding the audience, creating valuable content, and leveraging the power of storytelling, startups can build a strong online presence, engage with their audience, and drive growth. As we move to the next chapter, we will explore strategies for customer engagement and retention, focusing on how startups can build lasting relationships with their customers.

Chapter 6 Summary

This chapter highlighted the importance of content marketing and the power of storytelling in building brand awareness and engaging with the audience. We discussed how to create valuable content and craft compelling narratives that resonate with customers.

Key Takeaways

- Value-Driven Content: Produce content that provides value and addresses audience needs.
- Engaging Stories: Use storytelling to create emotional connections and humanize your brand.
- Consistent Distribution: Share content through various channels to reach your target audience effectively.

Chapter 7: Customer Engagement and Retention

In the competitive landscape of startups, acquiring new customers is important, but retaining them is crucial for long-term success. Customer engagement and retention strategies help build loyalty, increase lifetime value, and create advocates for the brand. This chapter will explore the principles of customer engagement, the importance of retention, and practical strategies to keep customers coming back.

Understanding Customer Engagement

Customer engagement is about creating meaningful interactions with customers that foster a positive experience and build a strong relationship. Engaged customers are more likely to be loyal, make repeat purchases, and recommend the brand to others. Key elements of customer engagement include:

1. Personalization: Tailoring the customer experience to meet individual needs and preferences. Personalization can be achieved through targeted content, personalized emails, product recommendations, and customized offers. Leveraging customer data and insights allows startups to deliver a more relevant and personalized experience.

   Personalization Examples:

   - Email Campaigns: Send personalized email campaigns based on customer behavior, preferences, and purchase history. For example, a fitness app could send workout recommendations tailored to the user's fitness goals and progress.
   - Product Recommendations: Use algorithms to suggest products or services that align with the customer's past purchases and browsing behavior.
   - Customized Offers: Provide exclusive discounts or offers based on the customer's loyalty or activity level.

2. Communication: Maintaining open and consistent communication with customers across multiple channels. This includes responding to inquiries promptly, providing updates on new products or services, and engaging with customers on social media. Effective communication helps build trust and keeps customers informed and connected.

   Communication Strategies:

   - Multi-Channel Approach: Use a combination of email, social media, live chat, and phone support to communicate with customers.

- Timely Responses: Ensure customer inquiries are addressed promptly, ideally within 24 hours.
- Regular Updates: Keep customers informed about new products, features, and promotions through newsletters and social media posts.

3. Value-Added Content: Providing content that adds value to the customer's experience. This could include educational blog posts, how-to guides, webinars, and exclusive access to resources. Value-added content positions the startup as a thought leader and helps customers see the brand as a valuable resource.

   Value-Added Content Examples:

- Educational Blog Posts: Create blog posts that offer tips, advice, and insights relevant to the customer's interests and needs. For example, a fitness app could publish articles on workout techniques, nutrition tips, and mental wellness.
- Webinars: Host live or recorded webinars featuring industry experts, product demonstrations, or in-depth discussions on relevant topics.
- Exclusive Resources: Provide access to exclusive resources such as eBooks, whitepapers, or premium content for loyal customers or subscribers.

4. Customer Feedback: Actively seeking and listening to customer feedback. This can be done through surveys, reviews, social media interactions, and direct conversations. Feedback provides insights into customer needs and pain points, allowing startups to improve their products and services.

   Customer Feedback Strategies:

- Surveys: Conduct regular surveys to gather feedback on customer satisfaction, product features, and service quality.

- Reviews and Testimonials: Encourage customers to leave reviews and share their experiences. Highlight positive testimonials on the website and social media.
- Direct Communication: Engage with customers through one-on-one interactions, such as phone calls or in-person meetings, to gather detailed feedback.

The Importance of Customer Retention

Customer retention is the practice of keeping existing customers engaged and satisfied so they continue to do business with the startup. Retaining customers is often more cost-effective than acquiring new ones and can significantly impact the startup's profitability. Here are some key benefits of customer retention:

1. Increased Lifetime Value: Loyal customers tend to make repeat purchases and spend more over time. By focusing on retention, startups can increase the average customer lifetime value (CLV), which contributes to long-term revenue growth.

   Example:

   A fitness app could offer subscription plans that incentivize long-term commitment, such as annual memberships with added benefits and discounts for renewals.

2. Reduced Acquisition Costs: Acquiring new customers can be expensive, involving significant marketing and sales efforts. Retaining existing customers reduces the need for constant acquisition, allowing startups to allocate resources more efficiently.

   Example:

Instead of spending heavily on advertising to acquire new users, a fitness app could invest in enhancing the user experience and offering loyalty rewards to keep existing users engaged.

3. Positive Word-of-Mouth: Satisfied customers are likely to recommend the brand to friends, family, and colleagues. Positive word-of-mouth can lead to organic growth and new customer acquisition without additional marketing expenses.

   Example:

   Encourage satisfied users to share their success stories on social media and offer referral bonuses for bringing in new users.

4. Competitive Advantage: High customer retention rates can provide a competitive advantage by creating a loyal customer base that is less likely to switch to competitors. This stability can be particularly valuable in highly competitive markets.

   Example:

   A fitness app could create a strong community aspect by hosting challenges, allowing users to connect and compete with friends, thereby fostering a sense of belonging and loyalty.

Strategies for Customer Engagement and Retention

To effectively engage and retain customers, startups need to implement a variety of strategies that focus on delivering exceptional experiences and building strong relationships. Here are some practical strategies:

1. Customer Onboarding: The onboarding process is the first opportunity to engage new customers and set the

tone for their experience. A well-designed onboarding process can help customers understand the product, access resources, and feel confident in their purchase.

Onboarding Tips:

- Welcome Messages: Send a personalized welcome email or message to new users.
- Tutorials and Guides: Provide easy-to-follow tutorials, guides, and videos to help users get started with the product.
- Check-Ins: Schedule follow-up emails or calls to check in with new users and address any questions or concerns.

2. Loyalty Programs: Implementing a loyalty program can incentivize repeat purchases and reward loyal customers. Loyalty programs can include points-based systems, exclusive discounts, early access to new products, and special perks. Recognizing and rewarding loyalty fosters a sense of appreciation and encourages continued engagement.

   Loyalty Program Examples:

   - Points System: Offer points for every purchase or activity, which can be redeemed for discounts or rewards.
   - Exclusive Offers: Provide loyal customers with access to special promotions, early product launches, or VIP events.
   - Tiered Rewards: Create different tiers of loyalty, with increasing benefits as customers reach higher levels of engagement.

3. Customer Support: Providing excellent customer support is crucial for retention. Startups should offer multiple channels for support, including email, chat, phone, and social media. Quick response times,

knowledgeable representatives, and proactive problem-solving contribute to a positive customer experience.

Customer Support Best Practices:

- Multi-Channel Support: Ensure customers can reach support through their preferred channel.
- Knowledge Base: Develop a comprehensive knowledge base or FAQ section to help customers find answers to common questions.
- Proactive Outreach: Reach out to customers proactively to check in and offer assistance, especially after a purchase or major update.

4. Community Building: Creating a community around the brand can enhance customer engagement and loyalty. This can be done through social media groups, online forums, events, and user-generated content campaigns. Communities provide a platform for customers to connect, share experiences, and feel part of a larger network.

   Community Building Strategies:

   - Social Media Groups: Create and manage groups on platforms like Facebook or LinkedIn where customers can engage with each other and the brand.
   - Online Forums: Host an online forum or community site where users can discuss topics, ask questions, and share tips.
   - Events and Meetups: Organize events, webinars, or meetups to bring the community together and strengthen relationships.

5. Personalized Offers and Recommendations: Using customer data to deliver personalized offers and product recommendations can enhance the customer experience. Personalized marketing messages and

tailored promotions show customers that the brand understands their needs and preferences.

Personalization Techniques:

- Behavioral Data: Use data on customer behavior and interactions to create personalized recommendations and offers.
- Segmentation: Segment the customer base into groups with similar characteristics and tailor marketing messages to each segment.
- Dynamic Content: Use dynamic content in emails and on the website to provide personalized experiences based on user data.

6. Regular Communication: Keeping customers informed and engaged through regular communication is essential. This includes email newsletters, product updates, and personalized messages. Regular communication helps maintain a connection with customers and keeps the brand top of mind.

Communication Strategies:

- Newsletters: Send regular newsletters with updates, tips, and exclusive content.
- Product Updates: Inform customers about new features, improvements, and upcoming releases.
- Personalized Messages: Send personalized messages on special occasions, such as birthdays or anniversaries, with exclusive offers or greetings.

7. Customer Appreciation: Showing appreciation for customers can strengthen relationships and build loyalty. This could include personalized thank-you notes, surprise gifts, and exclusive access to events or

promotions. Small gestures of appreciation can make a big impact on customer satisfaction.

Customer Appreciation Ideas:

- Thank-You Notes: Send personalized thank-you notes or emails after a purchase or milestone.
- Surprise Gifts: Offer surprise gifts or discounts to loyal customers as a token of appreciation.
- Exclusive Access: Provide exclusive access to special events, product launches, or promotions for loyal customers.

Measuring Engagement and Retention

To ensure that engagement and retention strategies are effective, startups need to track and measure key metrics. Some important metrics to monitor include:

1. Customer Retention Rate: The percentage of customers who continue to do business with the startup over a specific period. A high retention rate indicates strong customer loyalty.
2. Customer Lifetime Value (CLV): The total revenue a startup can expect from a customer over the course of their relationship. Increasing CLV is a key goal of retention strategies.
3. Net Promoter Score (NPS): A measure of customer satisfaction and loyalty based on the likelihood of customers recommending the brand to others. A high NPS indicates positive customer experiences and strong word-of-mouth potential.
    - Promoters: Customers who rate their likelihood of recommending the brand as 9 or 10.
    - Detractors: Customers who rate their likelihood of recommending the brand as 6 or lower.

4. Churn Rate: The percentage of customers who stop doing business with the startup over a specific period. Reducing churn is critical for improving retention.

5. Engagement Metrics: Metrics such as email open rates, click-through rates, social media interactions, and website visits provide insights into customer engagement levels.

Engagement Metrics to Track:

- Email Open Rates: The percentage of recipients who open an email.
- Click-Through Rates (CTR): The percentage of recipients who click on a link within an email.
- Social Media Interactions: The number of likes, shares, comments, and other interactions on social media posts.
- Website Visits: The number of visits to the website and the behavior of visitors on the site.

In Conclusion

Customer engagement and retention are essential components of a successful startup strategy. By understanding the importance of these elements and implementing practical strategies to engage and retain customers, startups can build lasting relationships, increase customer lifetime value, and drive long-term growth. As we move forward, we will explore growth hacking strategies that startups can use to achieve rapid and scalable growth.

Chapter 7 Summary

We focused on strategies for engaging and retaining customers, emphasizing the importance of personalized experiences, effective communication, and value-added content. The chapter also covered loyalty programs, excellent customer support, and building a community.

Key Takeaways

- Personalization: Tailor experiences to meet individual customer needs and preferences.
- Loyalty Programs: Implement programs to incentivize repeat purchases and reward loyalty.
- Community Building: Foster a sense of community around your brand to enhance engagement.

Chapter 8: Growth Hacking for Startups

In the fast-paced and competitive world of startups, traditional marketing strategies may not be sufficient to achieve rapid growth. Growth hacking offers an innovative approach to achieving scalable growth quickly by leveraging creative, low-cost tactics. This chapter will delve into the principles of growth hacking, key techniques, and how startups can implement a growth hacking mindset to drive exponential growth.

Understanding Growth Hacking

Growth hacking is a data-driven approach to achieving rapid growth by experimenting with various marketing tactics and optimizing them for maximum impact. The term "growth hacking" was coined by Sean Ellis in 2010, emphasizing the need for startups to focus on growth as their primary objective. Growth hacking combines marketing, data analysis, and product development to create strategies that drive customer acquisition, retention, and revenue.

Key Principles of Growth Hacking:

1. Data-Driven Decision Making: Growth hackers rely on data to inform their strategies and measure success. By tracking key metrics and analyzing user behavior, startups can identify what works and what doesn't, allowing for continuous optimization and improvement.

   Data-Driven Techniques:

   - A/B Testing: Conduct experiments by comparing two versions of a marketing element (e.g., landing pages, email subject lines) to see which performs better.
   - Analytics Tools: Use tools like Google Analytics, Mixpanel, and Amplitude to track user behavior and measure the effectiveness of growth tactics.

2. Creativity and Experimentation: Growth hacking involves thinking outside the box and experimenting with unconventional tactics. This could include viral marketing campaigns, leveraging social media trends, or optimizing user onboarding processes. The goal is to find innovative ways to drive growth without relying on traditional marketing methods.

   Creative Growth Hacks:

   - Viral Loops: Create features that encourage users to invite others, such as referral programs or social sharing incentives.
   - Gamification: Implement gamified elements like leaderboards, badges, and rewards to increase user engagement and retention.

- Content Marketing: Produce high-quality, shareable content that attracts organic traffic and backlinks.

3. Agility and Speed: Growth hacking requires a fast-paced and agile approach. Startups need to quickly implement and test new ideas, iterate based on feedback, and scale successful tactics. Speed is essential to stay ahead of competitors and capitalize on opportunities.

   Agile Practices:

   - Short Iteration Cycles: Develop and test new ideas in short cycles to quickly learn what works.
   - Rapid Prototyping: Create and test prototypes of new features or marketing campaigns to gather user feedback before full-scale implementation.

4. Customer-Centric Focus: Understanding the target audience and their needs is crucial for effective growth hacking. By putting the customer at the center of the strategy, startups can create personalized experiences that drive engagement and loyalty.

   Customer-Centric Strategies:

   - User Feedback: Continuously gather and analyze user feedback to identify pain points and opportunities for improvement.
   - Personalization: Use data to tailor marketing messages, product recommendations, and user experiences to individual preferences.

Key Growth Hacking Techniques

There are numerous growth hacking techniques that startups can use to achieve rapid growth. Here are some of the most effective ones:

1. Viral Marketing: Creating content or campaigns that encourage users to share with their networks can drive exponential growth. This could include viral videos, referral programs, or social media challenges. The key is to create something highly shareable that resonates with the target audience.

   Viral Marketing Examples:

   - Referral Programs: Offer incentives for users to refer friends, such as discounts, free products, or exclusive access.
   - Social Media Challenges: Launch challenges that encourage user participation and sharing, such as fitness challenges or photo contests.

2. Product-Led Growth: Leveraging the product itself to drive growth is a powerful technique. This could involve offering a freemium model, where users can access basic features for free and upgrade to premium features. By providing value through the product, startups can attract and retain users organically.

   Product-Led Growth Strategies:

   - Freemium Model: Offer a free tier with essential features and premium tiers with advanced features.
   - In-App Referrals: Integrate referral mechanisms within the product to encourage users to invite others.

3. A/B Testing: Continuously testing different variations of marketing messages, website designs, and product features can help identify what works best. A/B testing allows startups to make data-driven decisions and optimize for higher conversion rates.

   A/B Testing Tips:

- Hypothesis-Driven Testing: Formulate hypotheses for each test and use data to validate or refute them.
- Iterative Testing: Conduct multiple rounds of testing to refine and optimize marketing elements.

4. Search Engine Optimization (SEO): Optimizing the website for search engines can drive organic traffic and increase visibility. This involves keyword research, on-page optimization, and building high-quality backlinks. SEO is a long-term strategy that can yield sustainable growth.

   SEO Best Practices:

- Keyword Research: Identify high-traffic, low-competition keywords relevant to the startup's products or services.
- On-Page SEO: Optimize title tags, meta descriptions, headers, and content for target keywords.
- Link Building: Earn backlinks from reputable websites through content marketing, guest blogging, and outreach.

5. Content Marketing: Creating valuable and engaging content can attract and retain customers. This could include blog posts, videos, infographics, and podcasts. Content marketing not only drives traffic but also establishes the startup as a thought leader in the industry.

   Content Marketing Tactics:

- Blogging: Regularly publish high-quality blog posts on topics relevant to the target audience.
- Video Content: Create and share video content, such as tutorials, product demos, and customer testimonials.

- Guest Posting: Contribute articles to reputable blogs and websites to reach a wider audience and build backlinks.

6. Social Media Marketing: Leveraging social media platforms to reach and engage with the target audience can drive growth. This involves creating shareable content, running targeted ads, and engaging with followers. Social media marketing can amplify the reach and impact of growth hacking efforts.

   Social Media Strategies:

- Influencer Partnerships: Collaborate with influencers who have a large and engaged following to promote the startup's products or services.
- User-Generated Content: Encourage users to create and share content related to the brand, such as reviews, testimonials, and social media posts.
- Targeted Ads: Use social media advertising to reach specific demographics and drive traffic to the website or app.

7. Email Marketing: Building and nurturing an email list can drive repeat engagement and conversions. This involves sending personalized and relevant content, promotions, and updates to subscribers. Email marketing is a cost-effective way to keep customers engaged and drive growth.

   Email Marketing Techniques:

- Segmentation: Divide the email list into segments based on user behavior, preferences, and demographics to send targeted messages.
- Automation: Use email automation to send timely and personalized messages, such as welcome emails, abandoned cart reminders, and re-engagement campaigns.

- A/B Testing: Test different subject lines, content, and CTAs to optimize email performance.

8. Influencer Marketing: Collaborating with influencers who have a large and engaged following can amplify the startup's reach. Influencers can create authentic content that promotes the startup's products or services, driving awareness and conversions.

   Influencer Marketing Tips:

- Identify Relevant Influencers: Choose influencers whose audience aligns with the startup's target market.
- Authentic Collaboration: Work with influencers to create genuine and relatable content that resonates with their followers.
- Track Performance: Monitor the impact of influencer campaigns using metrics such as reach, engagement, and conversions.

Implementing a Growth Hacking Mindset

To successfully implement growth hacking, startups need to adopt a growth hacking mindset. This involves fostering a culture of experimentation, collaboration, and continuous learning. Here are some key steps to implement a growth hacking mindset:

1. Build a Growth Team: Assemble a cross-functional team with skills in marketing, data analysis, product development, and design. This team should work together to identify growth opportunities, experiment with new tactics, and optimize for success.

   Growth Team Roles:

- Growth Lead: Oversees the growth strategy and coordinates team efforts.
- Data Analyst: Analyzes data to identify trends, measure performance, and inform decisions.
- Marketing Specialist: Develops and executes marketing campaigns to drive growth.
- Product Manager: Focuses on product development and optimization to enhance user experience.
- Designer: Creates visual assets and ensures a seamless user experience.

2. Set Clear Goals and Metrics: Define specific growth objectives and key performance indicators (KPIs) to measure success. This could include metrics such as customer acquisition cost (CAC), lifetime value (LTV), conversion rates, and churn rates. Clear goals and metrics provide direction and focus for growth hacking efforts.

   Example Growth Objectives:

   - Increase User Acquisition: Achieve a 20% increase in new user sign-ups within the next three months.
   - Improve Conversion Rates: Increase the website's conversion rate by 15% through A/B testing and optimization.
   - Reduce Churn: Decrease the monthly churn rate by 10% through improved onboarding and customer support.

3. Embrace a Test-and-Learn Approach: Encourage a culture of experimentation where ideas are tested, measured, and iterated upon. This involves running small-scale experiments, analyzing the results, and scaling successful tactics. Failure should be viewed as a learning opportunity rather than a setback.

Testing Framework:

- Hypothesize: Formulate a hypothesis based on insights and assumptions.
- Experiment: Design and execute experiments to test the hypothesis.
- Analyze: Measure the results and determine whether the hypothesis is validated.
- Iterate: Refine the approach based on findings and conduct further tests if necessary.

4. Leverage Data and Analytics: Use data to inform decision-making and measure the impact of growth hacking efforts. This involves tracking key metrics, analyzing user behavior, and using tools such as Google Analytics, Mixpanel, and Amplitude. Data-driven insights are essential for optimizing growth strategies.

   Data Analysis Tips:

   - Track User Journeys: Monitor how users interact with the product from acquisition to retention to identify drop-off points and opportunities for improvement.
   - Cohort Analysis: Analyze user behavior over time to understand retention trends and the impact of changes.
   - Segmentation: Segment data by user demographics, behaviors, and acquisition channels to identify patterns and opportunities.

5. Focus on the Customer: Keep the customer at the center of all growth hacking efforts. This involves understanding their needs, preferences, and pain points, and creating personalized experiences that drive engagement and loyalty. Customer feedback should be continuously gathered and used to inform growth strategies.

Customer-Centric Practices:

- User Feedback: Collect feedback through surveys, interviews, and user testing to gain insights into customer needs and preferences.
- Customer Journey Mapping: Map out the customer journey to identify key touchpoints and optimize the user experience.
- Personalization: Use data to deliver personalized marketing messages, product recommendations, and user experiences.

6. Scale Successful Tactics: Once a growth hacking tactic has proven successful, scale it to maximize impact. This involves investing resources to amplify the reach and effectiveness of the tactic, whether it's through increased ad spend, expanded content creation, or enhanced product features.

   Scaling Strategies:

- Resource Allocation: Allocate budget and resources to scale successful tactics, such as increasing ad spend for high-performing campaigns.
- Process Optimization: Streamline and automate processes to efficiently scale growth efforts.
- Partnerships: Collaborate with partners and influencers to expand reach and amplify the impact of growth tactics.

In Conclusion

Growth hacking offers startups a powerful approach to achieving rapid and scalable growth. By embracing a data-driven, creative, and customer-centric mindset, startups can implement effective growth hacking techniques and drive exponential growth. As we move to the next chapter, we will explore analytics and performance measurement, focusing on how startups can track and analyze their marketing efforts to optimize for success.

Chapter 8 Summary

This chapter introduced growth hacking as a data-driven approach to achieving rapid growth through creative, low-cost tactics. We explored various growth hacking techniques and the importance of a customer-centric focus, agility, and continuous experimentation.

Key Takeaways

- Innovative Tactics: Experiment with unconventional marketing tactics to drive rapid growth.
- Data-Driven Insights: Use data to inform decisions and optimize strategies.
- Customer Focus: Prioritize understanding and meeting customer needs to drive engagement and loyalty.

Chapter 9: Analytics and Performance Measurement

In the world of startups, making informed decisions is crucial for success. Analytics and performance measurement provide the insights needed to understand the effectiveness of marketing efforts, identify areas for improvement, and optimize strategies for growth. This chapter will explore the importance of analytics, the key metrics to track, and the tools and techniques startups can use to measure and analyze performance.

The Importance of Analytics

Analytics involves the systematic collection, analysis, and interpretation of data to make informed decisions. For startups, analytics is essential for several reasons:

1. Data-Driven Decision Making: Analytics enables startups to make decisions based on data rather than intuition. This leads to more accurate and effective strategies, reducing the risk of costly mistakes.
2. Performance Measurement: By tracking key performance indicators (KPIs), startups can measure the success of their marketing efforts and understand what works and what doesn't. This allows for continuous improvement and optimization.
3. Customer Insights: Analytics provides valuable insights into customer behavior, preferences, and needs. This helps startups tailor their products, services, and marketing messages to better meet customer expectations.
4. Resource Allocation: Understanding the effectiveness of different marketing channels and campaigns allows startups to allocate resources more efficiently, maximizing return on investment (ROI).

Key Metrics to Track

There are numerous metrics that startups can track to measure the performance of their marketing efforts. Here are some of the most important ones:

1. Website Traffic: The number of visitors to the startup's website. This metric provides insights into the reach and visibility of marketing efforts. Key aspects to track include total visits, unique visitors, and traffic sources.

   Website Traffic Metrics:

   - Total Visits: The total number of visits to the website over a specific period.
   - Unique Visitors: The number of distinct individuals visiting the website.

- Traffic Sources: The origins of website traffic, such as organic search, direct, referral, and social media.

2. Conversion Rate: The percentage of website visitors who complete a desired action, such as making a purchase or signing up for a newsletter. A high conversion rate indicates that the website is effectively converting visitors into customers or leads.

   Conversion Rate = (Number of Conversions / Total Number of Visitors)×100

3. Customer Acquisition Cost (CAC): The total cost of acquiring a new customer, including marketing and sales expenses. Lowering CAC is essential for improving profitability.

   CAC = Total Marketing and Sales Expenses / Number of new customers acquired

4. Customer Lifetime Value (CLV): The total revenue a startup can expect from a customer over the course of their relationship. Increasing CLV is crucial for long-term growth and sustainability.

   CLV = Average Purchase Value × Average Purchase Frequency × Customer Lifespan

5. Churn Rate: The percentage of customers who stop doing business with the startup over a specific period. Reducing churn is important for maintaining a stable customer base and achieving sustainable growth.

   Churn Rate = (Number of Customers Lost During Period / Number of Customers at Start of Period) × 100

6. Engagement Metrics: Metrics such as email open rates, click-through rates (CTR), social media likes, shares, comments, and time spent on the website provide insights into customer engagement and the effectiveness of content and campaigns.

   Engagement Metrics:

- Email Open Rates: The percentage of recipients who open an email.
- Click-Through Rates (CTR): The percentage of recipients who click on a link within an email.
- Social Media Interactions: The number of likes, shares, comments, and other interactions on social media posts.
- Time Spent on Site: The average amount of time visitors spend on the website.

7. Return on Investment (ROI): The financial return generated from marketing efforts relative to the cost. Calculating ROI helps startups understand the profitability of their marketing activities and make informed investment decisions.

   ROI = ([Revenue from Marketing Activities – Marketing Costs] / Marketing Costs) ×100

8. Net Promoter Score (NPS): A measure of customer satisfaction and loyalty based on the likelihood of customers recommending the brand to others. A high NPS indicates positive customer experiences and strong word-of-mouth potential.

   NPS = % Promoters – % Detractors

- Promoters: Customers who rate their likelihood of recommending the brand as 9 or 10.
- Detractors: Customers who rate their likelihood of recommending the brand as 6 or lower.

Tools and Techniques for Analytics

There are various tools and techniques that startups can use to measure and analyze performance. Here are some of the most commonly used ones:

1. Google Analytics: A powerful and widely used tool for tracking website traffic, user behavior, and conversion rates. Google Analytics provides detailed insights into how visitors interact with the website, allowing startups to optimize their online presence.

   Google Analytics Features:

   - Audience Reports: Understand demographics, interests, and behaviors of website visitors.
   - Acquisition Reports: Analyze how users arrive at the website through different channels.
   - Behavior Reports: Track user interactions with the website, including page views and navigation paths.
   - Conversion Reports: Measure the effectiveness of conversion goals and e-commerce performance.

2. CRM Systems: Customer relationship management (CRM) systems such as Salesforce, HubSpot, and Zoho CRM help startups track customer interactions, manage leads, and measure the effectiveness of sales and marketing efforts.

   CRM Features:

   - Lead Management: Track and manage leads throughout the sales funnel.
   - Customer Profiles: Store detailed information about customers and their interactions with the company.
   - Sales Analytics: Analyze sales performance, pipeline stages, and revenue forecasts.
   - Marketing Automation: Automate email campaigns, lead scoring, and follow-up tasks.

3. Email Marketing Platforms: Tools like Mailchimp, Constant Contact, and Sendinblue provide analytics on email campaigns, including open rates, click-through

rates, and conversion rates. These insights help optimize email marketing strategies.

Email Marketing Features:

- Campaign Reports: Track the performance of individual email campaigns, including delivery rates and engagement metrics.
- A/B Testing: Test different email variations to determine the most effective content and design.
- Segmentation: Create targeted email lists based on user behavior and demographics.
- Automation: Set up automated email sequences for onboarding, re-engagement, and follow-ups.

4. Social Media Analytics: Platforms like Facebook Insights, Twitter Analytics, and LinkedIn Analytics provide data on social media performance, including engagement metrics, audience demographics, and reach. Social media management tools like Hootsuite and Buffer offer additional analytics capabilities.

   Social Media Analytics Features:

   - Engagement Metrics: Track likes, shares, comments, and other interactions on social media posts.
   - Audience Insights: Understand the demographics and interests of social media followers.
   - Content Performance: Analyze the effectiveness of different types of content and posting schedules.
   - Competitive Analysis: Compare social media performance with competitors and industry benchmarks.

5. A/B Testing Tools: Tools like Optimizely, VWO, and Google Optimize allow startups to conduct A/B tests on their websites, landing pages, and email campaigns. A/

B testing helps identify the most effective variations and optimize for better performance.

A/B Testing Features:

- Experiment Design: Create and launch A/B tests with different variations of web pages or emails.
- Statistical Analysis: Analyze test results to determine statistical significance and identify winning variations.
- Personalization: Use test insights to create personalized experiences for different user segments.
- Integration: Integrate A/B testing tools with analytics and CRM platforms for comprehensive data analysis.

6. Heatmaps and User Behavior Tools: Tools like Hotjar, Crazy Egg, and Mouseflow provide heatmaps, session recordings, and user feedback to understand how visitors interact with the website. These insights help improve user experience and conversion rates.

   Heatmap and User Behavior Features:

   - Heatmaps: Visualize user interactions on web pages, including clicks, scrolls, and mouse movements.
   - Session Recordings: Watch recordings of user sessions to see how visitors navigate the website.
   - Surveys and Polls: Collect user feedback through on-site surveys and polls.
   - Funnel Analysis: Identify drop-off points in the conversion funnel and optimize user journeys.

7. Dashboard and Reporting Tools: Tools like Tableau, Data Studio, and Klipfolio allow startups to create customized dashboards and reports that consolidate

data from multiple sources. This provides a comprehensive view of performance and helps in data-driven decision making.

Dashboard and Reporting Features:

- Custom Dashboards: Create interactive dashboards that display key metrics and performance indicators.
- Data Integration: Connect data from various sources, including analytics tools, CRM systems, and social media platforms.
- Visualization: Use charts, graphs, and tables to visualize data and identify trends.
- Automated Reports: Schedule and automate the generation of reports for regular performance updates.

Implementing an Analytics Strategy

To effectively leverage analytics, startups need to implement a structured approach. Here are key steps to developing an analytics strategy:

1. Define Objectives and KPIs: Start by defining clear objectives and key performance indicators (KPIs) that align with the startup's goals. This provides direction and focus for the analytics efforts.

   Example Objectives and KPIs:

   - Objective: Increase website conversions by 20% in six months.
   - KPIs: Conversion rate, bounce rate, average session duration, conversion funnel drop-off rate.

2. Set Up Tracking and Measurement: Use the appropriate tools and techniques to set up tracking and measurement for the defined KPIs. This involves implementing tracking codes, setting up goals and events, and integrating data sources.

   Tracking Setup Steps:

   - Implement Tracking Codes: Add Google Analytics tracking code to all web pages.
   - Set Up Goals: Define conversion goals in Google Analytics, such as form submissions and product purchases.
   - Event Tracking: Use event tracking to measure user interactions, such as button clicks and video plays.
   - Data Integration: Integrate analytics tools with CRM, email marketing, and social media platforms for comprehensive data collection.

3. Collect and Analyze Data: Continuously collect data and analyze it to gain insights into performance. This involves regularly reviewing dashboards and reports, identifying trends and patterns, and conducting deeper analysis as needed.

   Data Analysis Techniques:

   - Trend Analysis: Identify trends in key metrics over time to understand performance changes.
   - Segmentation Analysis: Segment data by user demographics, behavior, and acquisition channels to uncover insights.
   - Correlation Analysis: Analyze the relationship between different metrics to identify potential causes and effects.

- Attribution Analysis: Determine the impact of different marketing channels and touchpoints on conversions.

4. Make Data-Driven Decisions: Use the insights gained from analytics to make informed decisions and optimize strategies. This could involve adjusting marketing tactics, reallocating resources, or refining messaging based on data.

   Data-Driven Decision Making Examples:

- Campaign Optimization: Use A/B test results to optimize ad copy and landing page designs for higher conversions.
- Resource Allocation: Allocate budget to high-performing marketing channels and reduce spend on underperforming ones.
- Messaging Refinement: Refine marketing messages based on user feedback and engagement data to improve relevance and impact.

5. Continuous Improvement: Analytics is an ongoing process. Continuously monitor performance, conduct experiments, and make iterative improvements based on data. This ensures that the startup remains agile and responsive to changing market conditions.

   Continuous Improvement Strategies:

- Regular Reviews: Schedule regular performance reviews to assess progress towards goals and identify areas for improvement.
- Experimentation: Continuously test new ideas and tactics to discover what works best.
- Feedback Loop: Establish a feedback loop with customers, team members, and partners to gather insights and suggestions for improvement.

- Benchmarking: Compare performance metrics with industry benchmarks to identify strengths and weaknesses.

In Conclusion

Analytics and performance measurement are essential for startups to make data-driven decisions, optimize marketing efforts, and achieve sustainable growth. By tracking key metrics, using the right tools, and implementing a structured analytics strategy, startups can gain valuable insights, improve performance, and drive success. As we move to the final chapter, we will explore strategies for scaling marketing efforts to support the startup's growth and expansion.

Chapter 9 Summary

We discussed the importance of analytics and performance measurement in making informed decisions and optimizing marketing efforts. The chapter covered key metrics to track, tools and techniques for analysis, and the steps to implement a structured analytics strategy.

Key Takeaways

- Key Metrics: Track essential metrics like conversion rates, customer acquisition cost, and lifetime value.
- Analytical Tools: Utilize tools like Google Analytics and CRM systems for comprehensive data analysis.
- Continuous Improvement: Regularly review performance data and make iterative improvements based on insights.

Chapter 10: Scaling Your Marketing Efforts

As a startup grows, scaling marketing efforts becomes crucial to support expansion and sustain momentum. Scaling involves increasing the capacity and reach of marketing activities to drive higher levels of customer acquisition, engagement, and revenue. This chapter will explore the strategies, processes, and considerations necessary for effectively scaling marketing efforts.

Understanding the Need for Scaling

Scaling marketing efforts is essential for several reasons:

1. Increased Market Reach: As the startup grows, it needs to reach a larger audience to sustain its growth trajectory. Scaling marketing efforts helps tap into new markets and customer segments.
2. Enhanced Brand Awareness: Building a strong brand presence requires consistent and widespread marketing activities. Scaling helps amplify the brand's visibility and recognition.
3. Optimized Customer Acquisition: Efficiently scaling marketing efforts allows startups to acquire new customers at a lower cost, improving overall profitability.
4. Sustainable Growth: A scalable marketing strategy ensures that the startup can maintain and accelerate its growth without encountering bottlenecks or resource constraints.

Strategies for Scaling Marketing Efforts

1. Automate Marketing Processes:
    - Marketing Automation Tools: Utilize marketing automation platforms like HubSpot, Marketo, or ActiveCampaign to streamline repetitive tasks such as email campaigns, social media posting, and lead nurturing. Automation helps save time, reduce errors, and ensure consistent execution.
    - Customer Relationship Management (CRM): Implement a robust CRM system to manage and analyze customer interactions and data. A CRM helps in personalizing marketing efforts at scale and improving customer retention.

    Marketing Automation Benefits:

    - Efficiency: Automation reduces manual effort and increases productivity.

- Consistency: Ensures consistent communication and follow-ups with leads and customers.
- Personalization: Enables personalized marketing at scale, enhancing customer experience.

2. Leverage Data and Analytics:
    - Data-Driven Insights: Continuously analyze marketing data to identify trends, patterns, and opportunities for optimization. Use insights to make informed decisions and refine strategies.
    - Advanced Analytics: Invest in advanced analytics tools and techniques such as predictive analytics, machine learning, and AI to gain deeper insights and anticipate customer behavior.

Data-Driven Strategies:

- Segmentation: Segment the audience based on behavior, preferences, and demographics to deliver targeted messages.
- Attribution Modeling: Understand the impact of different marketing channels and touchpoints on conversions.
- Predictive Analytics: Use predictive models to forecast customer behavior and optimize marketing efforts.

3. Expand Digital Marketing Channels:
    - Content Marketing: Scale content marketing efforts by producing a diverse range of content formats, such as videos, podcasts, webinars, and infographics. Repurpose existing content to maximize reach and impact.
    - Social Media: Expand presence on multiple social media platforms to reach a broader

audience. Use targeted ads and influencer partnerships to amplify reach and engagement.

- SEO and SEM: Invest in search engine optimization (SEO) and search engine marketing (SEM) to drive organic and paid traffic. Scaling SEO involves creating high-quality content, building backlinks, and optimizing for local and mobile search.

Channel Expansion Tips:

- Content Calendar: Develop a content calendar to plan and schedule content across different channels.
- Platform-Specific Strategies: Tailor content and engagement strategies to each social media platform's unique audience and features.
- SEO Best Practices: Continuously optimize website content, structure, and technical aspects to improve search rankings.

4. Invest in Talent and Resources:

- Build a Skilled Team: Hire marketing professionals with expertise in areas such as digital marketing, content creation, analytics, and automation. A skilled team can execute and scale marketing strategies effectively.
- Outsource and Collaborate: Partner with agencies, freelancers, and industry experts to access specialized skills and resources. Collaboration can help scale efforts without overextending internal teams.

Talent and Resource Strategies:

- Training and Development: Invest in ongoing training and development programs to keep the marketing team updated with the latest trends and skills.

- Agency Partnerships: Collaborate with marketing agencies to leverage their expertise and resources for specific projects or campaigns.
- Freelancers: Use freelancers for tasks that require specialized skills or for temporary increases in workload.

5. Optimize Marketing Budget:

   - Performance-Based Budgeting: Allocate budget based on the performance and ROI of different marketing channels and campaigns. Continuously monitor and adjust spending to maximize impact.
   - Test and Scale: Start with small-scale experiments to test new ideas and strategies. Scale successful experiments by increasing investment and expanding reach.

   Budget Optimization Techniques:

   - Cost-Benefit Analysis: Regularly evaluate the cost-effectiveness of marketing activities and reallocate budget to high-performing areas.
   - ROI Tracking: Track the return on investment for each marketing channel to make data-driven budgeting decisions.
   - Pilot Programs: Implement pilot programs to test new marketing initiatives before scaling them.

6. Enhance Customer Experience:

   - Personalization: Use customer data to deliver personalized experiences across all touchpoints. Personalization at scale involves dynamic content, targeted messaging, and customized offers.

- Customer Support: Scale customer support by implementing self-service options such as chatbots, knowledge bases, and FAQ sections. Providing timely and efficient support enhances customer satisfaction and loyalty.

Customer Experience Enhancements:

- Dynamic Content: Use dynamic content on websites and emails to personalize the user experience based on behavior and preferences.
- Self-Service Tools: Implement chatbots and AI-driven customer support tools to provide instant assistance and answers to common questions.
- Feedback Mechanisms: Regularly collect and analyze customer feedback to identify areas for improvement and enhance the overall experience.

7. Expand Geographic Reach:

- International Marketing: Consider expanding into new geographic markets to reach a global audience. This involves localizing marketing content, understanding cultural nuances, and complying with local regulations.
- Partnerships and Alliances: Form strategic partnerships with local businesses, influencers, and industry associations to gain market insights and establish a presence in new regions.

Geographic Expansion Strategies:

- Market Research: Conduct thorough market research to understand the demand, competition, and regulatory environment in new regions.

- Localization: Adapt marketing content and campaigns to align with local languages, cultures, and preferences.
- Strategic Partnerships: Collaborate with local partners to leverage their market knowledge and establish credibility.

Processes for Effective Scaling

1. Standardize and Document Processes:
    - SOPs and Playbooks: Develop standard operating procedures (SOPs) and playbooks for key marketing activities. Documenting processes ensures consistency and efficiency as the team grows.
    - Training and Onboarding: Provide comprehensive training and onboarding programs for new team members. Ensuring that everyone understands the processes and tools used helps maintain quality and performance.

    Standardization Benefits:

    - Consistency: Standardized processes ensure consistent execution of marketing activities.
    - Efficiency: Documented procedures streamline onboarding and training, reducing the learning curve for new team members.
    - Quality Control: Standardization helps maintain high standards and minimize errors.
2. Implement Scalable Technologies:
    - Marketing Platforms: Use scalable marketing platforms that can handle increased volume and complexity. Cloud-based solutions offer flexibility and scalability.

- Integration: Ensure that marketing tools and platforms are integrated for seamless data flow and coordination. Integration enhances efficiency and provides a unified view of marketing performance.

Scalable Technology Strategies:

- Cloud-Based Solutions: Choose cloud-based marketing platforms that can scale with the startup's growth and offer robust features.
- API Integrations: Integrate different marketing tools through APIs to ensure smooth data transfer and automation.
- Scalability Testing: Regularly test the scalability of marketing technologies to ensure they can handle increased workloads.

3. Continuous Improvement and Optimization:

- Regular Reviews: Conduct regular performance reviews and audits to assess the effectiveness of marketing strategies and processes. Identify areas for improvement and implement changes promptly.
- Feedback Loop: Establish a feedback loop with customers, team members, and partners to gather insights and suggestions. Continuous feedback helps refine and optimize marketing efforts.

Continuous Improvement Practices:

- Performance Audits: Conduct periodic audits of marketing activities to evaluate effectiveness and identify improvement areas.
- Feedback Collection: Regularly collect feedback from customers and team members to understand pain points and opportunities.

- Iterative Optimization: Continuously optimize marketing strategies based on performance data and feedback to achieve better results.

Considerations for Scaling

1. Maintaining Quality and Consistency: As marketing efforts scale, it's crucial to maintain the quality and consistency of messaging and customer experience. Ensure that brand guidelines are followed and that customer interactions remain positive.

   Quality Maintenance Tips:

   - Brand Guidelines: Develop and enforce comprehensive brand guidelines to ensure consistency across all marketing materials.
   - Quality Assurance: Implement quality assurance processes to review and approve marketing content before publication.
   - Customer Feedback: Use customer feedback to monitor and improve the quality of marketing efforts.

2. Managing Costs: Scaling marketing efforts can lead to increased costs. Monitor expenses closely and ensure that scaling efforts are cost-effective and sustainable.

   Cost Management Strategies:

   - Budget Monitoring: Regularly track marketing expenses and compare them to budgeted amounts.
   - Cost-Benefit Analysis: Evaluate the cost-effectiveness of different marketing activities and adjust spending accordingly.
   - Resource Allocation: Allocate resources strategically to high-impact marketing initiatives.

3. Adapting to Market Changes: Stay agile and responsive to changes in the market environment, customer preferences, and competitive landscape. Being adaptable helps capitalize on new opportunities and mitigate risks.

   Market Adaptation Tips:

   - Trend Monitoring: Continuously monitor industry trends and market changes to identify new opportunities.
   - Agile Marketing: Adopt an agile marketing approach that allows for rapid adjustments to strategies and tactics.
   - Competitive Analysis: Regularly analyze competitor activities and market positioning to stay ahead of the competition.

In Conclusion

Scaling marketing efforts is a critical component of a startup's growth strategy. By automating processes, leveraging data and analytics, expanding digital channels, investing in talent and resources, optimizing the marketing budget, enhancing customer experience, and expanding geographic reach, startups can achieve sustainable and scalable growth. Implementing standardized processes, scalable technologies, and continuous improvement practices ensures that scaling efforts are efficient and effective. As the startup continues to grow, maintaining quality, managing costs, and adapting to market changes will be essential for long-term success.

Chapter 10 Summary

The final chapter focused on strategies for scaling marketing efforts to support startup growth. We covered automating processes, leveraging data, expanding digital channels, investing in talent, and optimizing budgets. Emphasis was placed on maintaining quality and adapting to market changes.

Key Takeaways

- Automation: Use marketing automation tools to streamline processes and ensure consistent execution.
- Data-Driven Scaling: Leverage data and analytics to optimize and scale marketing strategies effectively.
- Adaptability: Stay agile and responsive to changes in the market and customer preferences

In summary

Marketing for startups is a unique challenge that requires a blend of creativity, strategic thinking, and adaptability. Unlike established companies with vast resources, startups must maximize limited budgets and leverage innovative approaches to gain traction in competitive markets. A crucial starting point for any startup is defining its brand. This involves understanding the core values, mission, and vision of the company, which then translates into a compelling brand narrative that resonates with the target audience. A well-defined brand creates a strong foundation for all marketing efforts and helps in building a loyal customer base.

Market research and analysis are indispensable for startups. Knowing the market landscape, understanding customer needs, and identifying competitors' strengths and weaknesses provide valuable insights that inform strategic decisions. Startups must utilize both primary and secondary research methods to gather data and transform it into actionable intelligence. This helps in creating targeted marketing campaigns that address the specific pain points of the audience, thereby enhancing engagement and conversion rates.

Strategic marketing planning is the next crucial step. This involves setting clear, measurable goals and developing a roadmap to achieve them. Startups should prioritize creating a robust marketing plan that outlines the target market segments, positioning strategies, and marketing mix elements—product, price, place, and promotion. Flexibility is key in this phase, as startups need to be agile and ready to pivot based on market feedback and emerging opportunities.

Digital marketing plays a pivotal role in the success of startups. The digital landscape offers a cost-effective way to reach a broad audience, and startups must leverage various channels such as social media, email marketing, and search engine optimization (SEO). Building a strong online presence through a well-designed website and engaging content is essential. Social media platforms, in particular, offer a unique opportunity for startups to build communities, interact with customers, and amplify their brand message.

Content marketing and storytelling are powerful tools for startups. Creating valuable, relevant content that addresses the audience's needs and interests can position a startup as a thought leader in its industry. Storytelling humanizes the brand and creates an emotional connection with the audience. Startups should focus on producing high-quality content that educates, entertains, and inspires, thereby fostering trust and loyalty among customers.

Customer engagement and retention are critical for long-term success. Startups must go beyond acquiring new customers and focus on building strong relationships with existing ones. This can be achieved through personalized marketing, excellent customer service, and loyalty programs. Engaging customers through regular communication, feedback loops, and community-building activities ensures that they remain connected and invested in the brand.

Growth hacking is a concept that resonates well with startups. It involves using creative, low-cost strategies to acquire and retain customers. Startups must experiment with various growth tactics, such as viral marketing campaigns, referral programs, and partnerships. The key is to test, measure, and iterate rapidly to find what works best. Successful growth hacking requires a mindset of continuous learning and adaptability.

Analytics and performance measurement are essential components of startup marketing. Startups need to track the performance of their marketing efforts using key metrics such as customer acquisition cost (CAC), lifetime value (LTV), conversion rates, and return on investment (ROI). Data-driven decision-making enables startups to optimize their marketing strategies, allocate resources efficiently, and achieve better results.

Scaling marketing efforts is the final piece of the puzzle. As startups grow, their marketing strategies need to evolve to support increased demand and broader market reach. This involves expanding marketing channels, investing in more sophisticated tools and technologies, and building a scalable marketing team. Startups should also focus on maintaining the quality and consistency of their brand message as they scale.

In conclusion, marketing for startups requires a dynamic and multifaceted approach. By defining a strong brand, conducting thorough market research, developing strategic plans, leveraging digital marketing, creating compelling content, engaging customers, employing growth hacking techniques, and using analytics for continuous improvement, startups can build a solid marketing foundation that drives growth and success

Notes, Books and Blog Sources

1. "The Lean Startup" by Eric Ries
2. "Traction: How Any Startup Can Achieve Explosive Customer Growth" by Gabriel Weinberg and Justin Mares
3. "Made to Stick: Why Some Ideas Survive and Others Die" by Chip Heath and Dan Heath
4. "Contagious: How to Build Word of Mouth in the Digital Age" by Jonah Berger
5. "Growth Hacker Marketing: A Primer on the Future of PR, Marketing, and Advertising" by Ryan Holiday
6. "Purple Cow: Transform Your Business by Being Remarkable" by Seth Godin
7. "Crossing the Chasm: Marketing and Selling High-Tech Products to Mainstream Customers" by Geoffrey A. Moore
8. "Blue Ocean Strategy: How to Create Uncontested Market Space and Make the Competition Irrelevant" by W. Chan Kim and Renée Mauborgne
9. "Building a StoryBrand: Clarify Your Message So Customers Will Listen" by Donald Miller
10. "Hooked: How to Build Habit-Forming Products" by Nir Eyal
11. "This Is Marketing: You Can't Be Seen Until You Learn to See" by Seth Godin
12. "Influence: The Psychology of Persuasion" by Robert B. Cialdini
13. "The Startup Owner's Manual: The Step-By-Step Guide for Building a Great Company" by Steve Blank and Bob Dorf
14. "The 22 Immutable Laws of Marketing: Violate Them at Your Own Risk!" by Al Ries and Jack Trout
15. "Top of Mind: Use Content to Unleash Your Influence and Engage Those Who Matter to You" by John Hall
16. "Killing Marketing: How Innovative Businesses Are Turning Marketing Cost into Profit" by Joe Pulizzi and Robert Rose
17. "Invisible Selling Machine" by Ryan Deiss
18. "Marketing Rebellion: The Most Human Company Wins" by Mark W. Schaefer

19. "The New Rules of Marketing and PR: How to Use Social Media, Online Video, Mobile Applications, Blogs, News Releases, and Viral Marketing to Reach Buyers Directly" by David Meerman Scott
20. "The Art of Startup Fundraising: Pitching Investors, Negotiating the Deal, and Everything Else Entrepreneurs Need to Know" by Alejandro Cremades
21. Philip Kotler: Renowned for his contributions to marketing, Kotler's principles emphasize the importance of understanding consumer behavior and strategic planning. Philip Kotler on Marketing
22. HubSpot Blog: URL: https://blog.hubspot.com/ Description: Provides in-depth articles on marketing, sales, and customer service with a focus on inbound marketing strategies.
23. Neil Patel's Blog: URL: https://neilpatel.com/blog/ Description: Offers comprehensive guides and tips on SEO, content marketing, and growth hacking tailored for startups and small businesses.
24. Content Marketing Institute: URL: https://contentmarketinginstitute.com/
    Description: A leading resource for content marketing strategies, insights, and best practices.
25. Moz Blog: URL: https://moz.com/blog
    Description: Provides articles, research, and tools focused on SEO and online marketing to help startups improve their online presence.
26. GrowthHackers: URL: https://growthhackers.com/
    Description: A community-driven site that shares insights, case studies, and strategies on growth hacking and startup marketing.
27. Copyblogger: URL: https://copyblogger.com/blog/
    Description: Focuses on content marketing, copywriting, and SEO to help startups create compelling content and attract audiences.
28. MarketingProfs: URL: https://www.marketingprofs.com/
    Description: Offers a variety of marketing resources, including articles, podcasts, and online courses, covering a wide range of marketing topics.
29. Kissmetrics Blog: URL: https://blog.kissmetrics.com/

Description: Provides data-driven marketing insights, focusing on analytics, conversion optimization, and customer engagement.

30. Buffer Blog: URL: https://buffer.com/resources
    Description: Shares social media marketing tips, strategies, and case studies to help startups build their online presence.
31. Entrepreneur Marketing Section: URL: https://www.entrepreneur.com/topic/marketing
    Description: Features articles and resources on a wide range of marketing topics, including digital marketing, branding, and growth strategies for startups.

Printed in Great Britain
by Amazon

60733636R00077